Swimhiking in the and North Eas

Second Edition

Peter Hayes

Published by

Gilbert Knowle Publishers
6 Valeside
Durham DH1 4RF
England

 ®

www.swimsac.co.uk

ISBN: 978-1-9998871-1-7

Preface to the First Edition

This book contains thirty two circular swimhikes in the Lake District and a further twelve in North East England. Alongside these routes are many questions of interest for a swimhiker: why are islands so nice and private islands immoral? Why is the view from the centre of a lake so good? Why are seagulls more terrifying than sharks? etc. I also give some account of my efforts so far to achieve fame and fortune with a swimsac.

Preface to the Second Edition

A few years ago, I crawled into the attic, groped in a box, pulled out very last copy of this book, and posted it off with a sigh of relief. 'Shall I bother to do some more'? I thought. 'No. It's too much hassle'. But then people complained—the Hampshire-Wrights particularly—and said I was lazy not to do another one, or at least bring the book back into print. So, as you see, I have yielded to public demand.

The main change to this edition is that I have drawn the approximate lines of the numbered routes on the maps. The text has been little altered. For the most part I have confined myself to correcting errors like getting east and west mixed up, which I seem to have done constantly. I have resisted the temptation to add further routes; I hope readers will be inspired to create new routes for themselves. I have, however, added some footnotes and extra sections, including some further information on the Frog Graham Round.

Peter Hayes, April 2018

Contents

5

INTRODUCTION

For thousands of years human beings have yearned to fly like birds. And now, thanks to the marvels of modern engineering we all can, for remarkably little cost, simply by buying an air ticket.

But we can't really. Trooping through the airport, squashing into the seats, sitting trapped and passive as the metal tube roars into the air: it is hard to imagine anything less like the flight of a bird. It is true that once the plane has broken through the clouds you can get a god-like view, but you have no connection to the landscape beneath, and most people remain firmly oblivious to it.

In pursuing the impossible dream of flying like a bird we have neglected another humbler animal hopping around at our feet who we really can imitate. The technology is simple, the cost is minimal, and it is probably just as much fun. We can all be like frogs.

A frog can cross land and water, and anyone who can swim can do the same. But a frog can do something else: it can *journey* over both land and water: it can swim down a river or across a lake, come out onto the land and keep right on going. Now, if we want to do that it all becomes rather difficult; we can get in at one side, and come out at another, true, but where are our shoes, our clothes, our food, our money? Swimming is wonderful, but it cannot form part of our journey; we are tied to the spot where we entered the water, because that is where we left our stuff.

There are different solutions to this problem. You can hire a boat to chug along behind you, but then it all becomes a bit of an expedition. Also, what about the people dawdling along in the boat, are they not going to become a little bored? A shared adventure undertaken amongst friends and equals is in danger of becoming rather one-sided. Of course, you can swim distances with an accompanying boat that you might not otherwise dare attempt, but just as it is more satisfying to climb Latrigg unaided than to climb Mount Everest with a bunch of Sherpas tagging along behind lugging enormous rucksacks full of Kendal Mintcake, so a boat means that you are no longer doing something entirely by your own efforts and at your own risk.

You can also have an elaborate system of drops—leave clothes at one end, walk back to the other, leave clothes at the other end swim across, get into your clothes, walk back to where you started and pick up the clothes you left. But then the very route of the hike is defined not by where you want to go, but by doglegs to deposit and pick up your things.

No, the simple, easy, obvious solution is to take your shoes, your clothes, your money, and whatever else, with you. And for that you need a swimmer's rucksack, or swimsac, which you can use equally well on land or on water.

'But' (I hear you say) 'I haven't got a swimsac'. Actually, if you are an outdoorsy sort of person you probably have got most if not all of the bits that make up a swimsac already, and if not you can easily get hold of them. All you have to do is put them together.

How to Make a Swimsac

A crude but effective swimsac is very simple to assemble. You need:

(1) A rucksack with two side pockets. The rucksack does not have to be waterproof, and in fact it is better if it is not.
(2) Two extra straps: (a) a waist strap and (b) an upper body strap (sternum strap). Depending on the rucksack you choose, one or both of these straps may already be in place. If it lacks the upper strap, or if the strap is uncomfortably narrow, you can either sew or tie a wider strap on to the shoulder straps.
(3) A drybag (a waterproof bag with a roll top). This is for clothes etc.
(4) A double chambered inflatable child's armband.

Cut the armband in half and put one half in each side pocket. Put the drybag in the rucksack and start hiking. When you reach water, put your shoes and clothes in the drybag, strap the whole thing on around your body and Hey Presto! You are ready to start swimming!*

'But '(I hear you say) 'I cannot be bothered to do all that. Why don't you do everything for me, stamp the word "swimsac" on the bag and sell it to me instead'? This is my plan,** though I still encourage you to make your own. There is no reason why a home made swimsac should not work perfectly well,

---

* To refine your sack you can punch holes in the side pockets for the valves of the armbands and a hole in the base of the outer rucksack so that it drains more easily. To make these holes you will need metal eyelets and washers together with a simple riveting device, looking a bit like a small stapler, which can be bought from a haberdashery. You can also rip out any padding in the rucksack that absorbs water.
** *Note to 2nd Edn* This plan has got nowhere.

and it is always very satisfying to use a piece of equipment that you have assembled for yourself.[*]

Using a Swimsac

A great advantage of a swimsac is that it leaks. At least, water leaks into the outer sac. This makes swimming more natural and enjoyable, it is not like paddling along with a balloon on your back, and on land the fabric is much more comfortable than if it were waterproof.

Because the outer sac leaks, divide what you carry into two categories: items which you want to stay dry like clothes, sandwiches and maps and items which can get wet like water bottles, apples, and compasses. Put the items to stay dry in the inner drybag and close it securely, folding the opening at least three times before buckling it shut. Items that can get wet can be put either in the main sac or in any spare pockets. If you want to use a waterproof container for valuables, put it in the drybag. Unless you are carrying bricks around with you do not worry about the weight of the sac.

It is helpful to have one or two plastic bags for things that you want to put in the drybag but which might be damp or dirty. These include your shoes or boots and, if its raining, the clothes that you are wearing.

On land a swimsac is carried over your shoulders exactly like a rucksack. When you enter the water take the shoulder straps *off* your shoulders and attach both the upper body strap and waist strap *underneath* your shoulders. With these two straps

---

[*] And if you happen to drown your lawyers will find it more difficult to argue that it was my fault.

A Swimsac

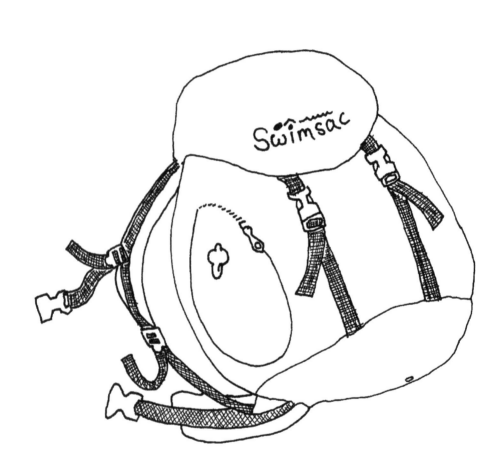

in place, you can comfortably swim any swimming stroke, front or back. The straps should be moderately firm but need not be tight in order to hold the sac in place. To swim on your back, rest the swimsac against your chest and stomach with the straps attached across your back. To switch from swimming from your front to swimming on your back, or visa versa, tread water and twist the sac though 180 degrees.

To help keep things dry, keep the swimsac high in the water. Never swim in a way that forces the swimsac underneath you.

As well as a swimsac you need three abilities in order to follow the swimhikes in this book. (1) You need to be able to walk. (2) You need to be able to navigate. The routes are based around checkpoints with suggested ways in between, not all of them on a path. Although there is doubtless some kind of hi-tech gadget that tells you exactly where you are and where to go, it is more in keeping with the low tech spirit of swimhiking to use a good old fashioned map and compass. (3) You need to feel at home swimming out of your depth in open water. This last point is rather important as the routes often take you right across the middle of a lake. However, it is possible to enjoy swimhiking without going out of your depth by alternating walking and swimming along the shoreline. In the Lake District there are some particularly pleasant stretches along the north west bank of Coniston Water and on both the east and western shores of Derwentwater, where it is easy to get in and out at any point. The sandy beaches of North East England, such as Druridge Bay and Seaburn, are also good for shoreline swimhiking.

Safety
Safety is your responsibility.

Maps
The maps I have drawn, excellent though they are, cannot be *wholly relied upon* to indicate some of the *finer features* of the terrain through which you will pass. For this you will need a topographic map. Four Ordnance Survey 1:25,000 maps (North East, North West, South East and South West) cover all the Lake District routes. Alternatively you can use the Harvey Maps. In the North East, the Ordnance Survey 1:50,000 maps are generally sufficient, but the 1:25,000 maps are better. All the maps in this book point north. The routes they cover are listed by number in the Contents.

Times
In the Contents the routes are classified as **s** for short (these took me under two hours) **m** for medium (two to four hours and **l** for long (four to six hours). When on land I ran, but not very fast. I generally swam breaststroke. Walkers and leisurely swimmers will take double these times, athletes will take half the time, but I do not want to encourage you to hurry, better to slow down and enjoy yourself.

Parking
I made elaborate notes about all the places you could park for each swimhike, but have decided not to include them: you can work it out for yourself, and in any event I am hoping that this information will soon become obsolete as the sun sets on a mountain of rusting motor vehicles and we return to horses and bicycles.

The Lake District

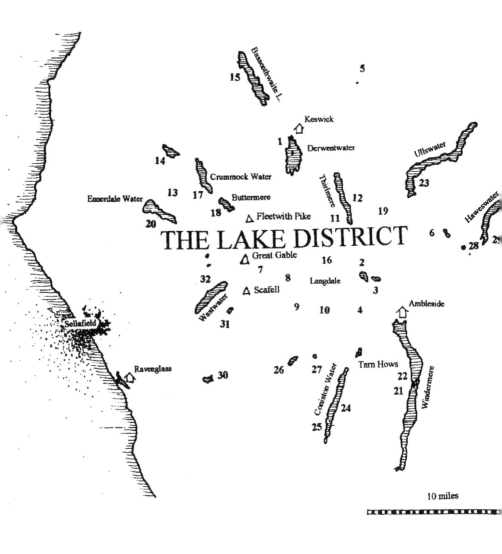

THE LAKE DISTRICT

Bassenthwaite L.

15

5

Keswick

1 Derwentwater

Ullswater

14

Crummock Water

23

Emerdale Water

13 17 Buttermere

Thirlmere

12

19

Haweswater

20

18 △ Fleetwith Pike

11

6

28

△ Great Gable

16

2

7

32 8 Langdale

3

△ Scafell

9 10 4

Ambleside

Wastwater

31

Sellafield

30

26 27 Coniston Water Tarn Hows

22

Ravenglass

Windermere

21

24

25

10 miles

THE LAKE DISTRICT

It is possible to swimhike anywhere there is land and water, but there are some places in the world that are especially favourable. The English Lake District is one of these places. Its mountains are delightful for walking and running over, its lakes and tarns are breathtaking for swimming across and when you join these activities together the Lakes becomes a paradise. In fact, not to do both is rather missing out. If you travel to the Lake District and merely look at the lakes but do not venture into them, it is rather as if you go there merely to look up at the mountains rather than to climb them. You might respond that you are climbing a mountain 'for the view', but this is a reductive explanation for why people enjoy hiking: there is a great deal of satisfaction to finding a summit cairn in thick fog. Even if you are hiking simply for the view, this only serves to emphasise what you are missing as the view from the centre of a lake is often rather better than from a high point.

Latrigg

River Derwent

Fitz Park

KESWICK

Moot Hall

Portinscale footbridge

Crow Park

Nichol End

carpark

Isthmus Bay

Lingholm

Cockshot Wood

Derwent Isle

Marshmallow I.

Strandshag Bay

Lord's I.

1

St. Herbert's I.

Calf Close Bay

Kitchen Bay

Rampsholme I.

Cat Bells

Otterbield I.

Victoria Bay

DERWENTWATER

Watendlath Jetty

1 mile

1. The Islands of Derwentwater

If you look down on the fat blue lake of Derwentwater from one of the encircling mountains you can see five enticing islands. Four of them are lined up roughly like stepping stones across the lake. How inviting to swim from one to the other!

But your first view of Derwentwater is unlikely to be from the top of a mountain. It is more likely that on a hot summer's day you join thousands of other car drivers in an interminable queue through Keswick's picturesque traffic flow system until you finally reach the Lakeshore carpark—the largest in the town—and by great good fortune or ruthlessly selfish manoeuvring secure a parking space. A few yards west of the cauldron of road rage in the carpark there is a very different atmosphere, a pleasant grassy meadow full of picnickers and children. And here is your first glimpse of Derwentwater! Do not be discouraged that from this angle the lake looks like a large and somewhat dirty duck pond. It warms up quickly in the summer as the brown shallow water absorbs the heat.

Continue on foot to Isthmus Bay, the entry point for the first swim. Change into your swimsuit, and put your clothes, shoes, wallet, map, sandwich and towel into your waterproof inner bag. An apple can go in the gap between the inner bag and outerbag. Fold the inner bag shut, strap down the hood of the outer bag, inflate the sidepockets, strap the bag around your chest, *but not over your shoulders* and then attach the waist strap.

Plunge in! When you do this for the first time it is hard not to be amazed that the swimsac, far from weighing you down is barely noticeable on your back, as the water bears the weight of the load.* As you swim you will discover that it is actually much more pleasant to have a pack on your back in the water than it is on land.

Strike out West for Nichol End; look for the moored boats. You will notice that the water, which at first tasted a little ducky, becomes much more pleasant and drinkable in the middle of the lake. Then as you approach Nichol End it starts to taste of engine oil. Exit onto the slipway.

Well done! You have crossed Derwentwater, albeit at a rather narrow point. The bulk of the route is now going to involve getting back again by swimming right across the middle of the lake, but with the four island stepping stones to help you on your way. Get changed and take the inland wooded path to Kitchen Bay. This bay extends south to one of the nicest areas of shoreline with grassy backs and knots of pines, and a little off shore the rocky outcrop of Otterbield Island, the first of the stepping stones.

Get changed back into your swimsuit again and leave your shoes at the top of the inner bag: they are all you will need for the islands. Swim to Otterbield, a tiny, delicate island with heather, flowers, and a single oak.

In the middle of the lake lies the next stepping stone, St. Herbert's Island. The swim gives you the best views of the surrounding fells. Before you set off, however, I should mention that unless you are absolutely confident of getting to the far shore, now is the time to turn back. You have already

---

* For a more technical explanation, see 'Swimsacs and the Laws of Physics' in the Appendix.

crossed the lake once and visited an island, there is no shame involved, and you have a very pleasant alternative route, which is to mix walking and swimming anticlockwise round Derwentwater's shore. This is far better than being marooned an involuntary hermit on St. Herbert's (or God forbid Rampsholme) until a passing boat takes pity on you.

The Herbert who once lived on Saint Herbert's Island, appears to have been one of the more boring of the saints. His only claim to fame is that after his friend St. Cuthbert prayed about the matter, God arranged for them both to die on exactly the same day, March 19th or 20th, in 687, or possibly 678.

Wordsworth writes:

Wilt thou behold this shapeless heap of stones,
The desolate ruins of St. Herbert's cell.
There stood his threshold; there was spread the roof
That sheltered him, a self-secluded man[*]

There is indeed a low ruin, like an old wall, to be seen in the undergrowth at the North side of the St. Herbert's Island, although there seems to be ambiguity over whether this was indeed his chapel and cell or just an old summer house. For the rest, after you have wormed your way between the holly bushes that ring the shore you will find tall trees of fir and of birch, a carpet of pine needles, a glade. Otterbield is a miniature jewel, but St. Herbert's has a spacious elegance offering shade and soft ground. Well might the perplexed poet have exclaimed of these two lovely places:

---

[*] William Wordsworth, *Inscription: For the spot where the hermitage stood on St. Herbert's Island, Derwentwater.*

Different in all but beauty—
That both share.
Who durst to call
The which is furthest fair?[*]

The contest for the most beautiful island on Derwentwater does not, unfortunately, extend to the final two islands to be visited. Rampsholme Island, the third stepping stone, is in many respects a slightly smaller version of St. Herbert's with one important difference: it has been colonised by shags and is consequently a little smelly. Lord's Island, the final island of the four, has suffered a worse fate: human beings. Of course, all of the islands, are visited by canoeists and other boaters, and if you are searching for a quiet campsite on a summer's evening you are apt to be disappointed. But perhaps because Lord's Island is so close to the shore it seems to have hosted more than its fair share of lumpen-canoeists, at least judging by the beer cans they have left there.

The swim from St. Herbert's to Rampsholme, and again from the spit at Rampsholme to Lord's Island, are both fairly substantial steps across the lake. The exit from Lord's Island is rather boggy and bushy, but once in the water it is a short hop to the beach at Strandshag Bay.

Congratulations! You have made it back to the mainland. Now you can return to the carpark through Cockshot Wood.

This double crossing by no means exhausts the charms of Derwentwater. A second natural line across the centre of the lake, the 'forty minute crossing', takes you from the Watendlath Jetty to Victoria Bay, with paths branching out at

---

[*] Actually, I made this up myself.

each end for any number of routes. All five main islands, including Derwent Isle* can be visited in a loop from Kitchen Bay, and there are other small islands to discover as well.

Boats on Derwentwater are generally sedate, although you should watch out for the passenger ferry that bowls purposefully along rather close to the shore, the waterborne equivalent of a grumpy bus driver.**

Islands
There is something especially charming about islands. None are ever quite the same; every island has its own special character. Complete and enclosed, everything must be found on the island. It is as though the world with all its infinite possibilities does not exist, or rather all the world must be found on the island, which is its own little world. This notion delights the imagination. Everything on the island is examined with a minute, almost hallucinogenic attention and its potential is magnified to the limit; a hillock becomes a mountain, a few trees a forest, a strand of pebbles a beach.

---

* Derwent Isle is owned by the National Trust, but it is only opened to the public for five days a year, and some of these days are apt to be cancelled when the water level is too low for the ferry. When I queried this curious arrangement, the friendly lady in the information booth explained that the island was rented out, and that the tenant paid 'a lot of money' to the Trust--presumably to keep members of the public at bay.

** *Note to 2nd Edn* After the first edition of this book came out, I did some swimhiking on telly. The most enjoyable of these occasions was at Derrwentwater with Katie Knapman for Countryfile. But when I looked to find footage of Katie and I on the internet, all I could track down was a rather stern article in the *Cumberland and Westmoreland Herald* (3rd July 2009) under the title: 'Program Failed to Warn of Dangers of Lake Swim'.

Behind the imaginative appeal of an island is a dim Adamite memory. The island recreates for us the Garden of Eden. Cut off from the sordid world it is a natural innocent place.

Unfortunately, the ancient memory of Eden evoked by an island is followed quickly by the desire to have the island all to oneself and to keep everyone else off with the help of a ferocious dog or a machine gun. The beauties of a natural world are things for human beings to share. No one has the right to own a uniquely beautiful place, and as all islands are unique, no one has a right to own an island. But men do own them, not by right but by force backed by law that favours the wealthy. Step onto an island, and soon a sibilant voice breathes a question in your ear.

'Are you rich'?

Most people, of course, answer 'No' and the conversation goes no further. But a few people answer 'Yes'.

'Then all this can be yours', whispers the voice seductively. 'You can be master of the island. King of the island. You can be God'.

It is no coincidence, therefore, that the owners of islands in literature, from Dr Moreau with his hideous experiments to Dr No with his man-eating octopus invariably turn out to be megalomaniacs. And in real life, it is notable that the appeal of owning an island is one that works especially powerfully on people who have leapt unashamed into a sticky vat of desires—fame, ruthless greed, lust—and have crawled out plastered with cash. So it is that islands are often owned by pop stars, slum landlords, and by the successful condom manufacturer and failed balloonist Sir Richard Branson.* It is as much for their own good as to uphold the rights of the rest of us that these people should be prevented from acting out their fantasies of island ownership, else who knows what they might get up to.

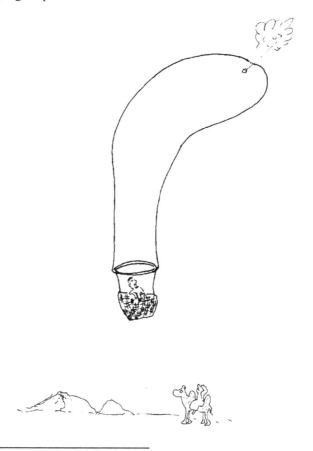

---

* The fact that Sir Richard Branson's balloons, when they were not floating away without him, kept on popping, should not be taken in any sense as an adverse comment on his brand of condoms, which are no doubt extremely reliable.

2. Alcock Tarn and Grasmere

What a charming village Grasmere is! The churchyard with Wordsworth's grave, the daffodils, the Green, the meandering Rothay, the cosy stone houses behind their wrought iron gates, each with the word 'Private' stamped in the middle. No wonder it gets crowded.

There are extensive parking possibilities for the thousands of tourists that are drawn to this honeypot, with an enormous car and coachpark at the Ambleside end; a 'premium rate' carpark next to the garden centre; a quaintly anachronistic lay-by with an honesty box beside the church, and, if you are cunning, various places to park for nothing at all at the north end of the village. In the summer all of them will be full. But let us assume that you have somehow parked your car, perhaps you have even walked or caught a bus. Leave the village, cross the A591 and clamber the steep path to the northwest end of Alcock Tarn. The tarn is shaped like a jellybaby. You enter at the stone on its right shoulder and swim down to its left foot, where there is a marvellous view over the valley. Alcock Tarn is ideal as a gentle introduction to swimhiking. It is generally rather shallow and as you are never more than a few yards from the bank, you would have to exercise considerable ingenuity to drown.

From Alcock Tarn follow the dramatic craggy path down to Wordsworth's home, Dove Cottage. At this point the swimhiking party divides into two. Those who are satisfied with having swum the length of the tarn can walk over White Moss Common—watch for deer—and then follow the River Rothay upstream to the path along the South West shore of Grasmere. Here they will meet up with their more amphibious companions who have swum Grasmere, east to west, via its unnamed island.

The only disadvantage to the swimming route is the entry point, a prickly scramble down from the main road. Once in the water exhilaration takes over. The first piece of excitement is the current. Although Grasmere is a considerable lake, there is a noticeable pull from the River Rothay as it flows north round the island towards its next destination of Rydal Water. It is, in truth, not a very powerful current, but it makes a change from a lake being totally still. Strike across the current to land beneath the overhanging branches of the island. This island is of enchanting beauty, with a delightful variety of trees, and a glade of grass that looks for all the world that it has been mowed. Could this really be the unaided work of God? Surely man has had a hand in it? But the map marks it as uncultivated land, and as we have seen from Derwentwater, the hand of man is usually manifested by the beer cans he discards.

From the southern tip of the island swim west to the shore and rejoin your companions who have chosen the walking route. If the party is short of time, you can now join the minor road back to Grasmere village, although this route holds little interest aside from the entertainment afforded by the fierce warning notices to non-customers posted outside the Faeryland Café. A more satisfying but longer route is to take the path above Hunting Stile and over Silver How before descending to the village.

A fitting conclusion to the hike is found in the village graveyard. Wordsworth's final resting place? No! It is Sarah Nelson's Grasmere Gingerbread Shop! On the walls of this quaint little shop is a tale to rival Hilary and Tensing nibbling Kendal Mintcake on the summit of Mount Everest. The story tells of how His Highness Prince Andrew once visited the

Lake District. In honour of the Prince's visit, the loyal and patriotic folk of the region had booked a village hall where they had prepared an elaborate feast of local produce: mutton, lamb, sheep's milk cheese, cumberland sausage, whole roasted sheep, etc. etc. Once the meal had been made ready and been laid out beautifully on a great table, everyone trooped outside and stood waiting expectantly, scanning the horizon and straining their ears for the distant 'wooba wooba' that would announce the arrival of the royal helicopter.

To the surprise and disappointment of all present, when Prince Andrew finally turned up—very late—he took *not a single bite of food* and only stayed for ten minutes before *urgent business* required him to get back in the royal helicopter and whisk away again. However, as he flew back over the fells, Prince Andrew managed to munch on Sarah Nelson's Grasmere Gingerbread. He pronounced it to be delicious.*

---

* *Note to 2nd Edn* This story has now been replaced by a rather dull item about Prince Charles. Let us hope that before too long it is replaced again with something on William and Kate or, better still, Harry and Meghan.

Lakes around Loughrigg

3. Rydal Water

Half a mile below Grasmere, Rydal Water is one of the smallest and shallowest of the lowland waters. It is, if possible, even more popular than Grasmere and on a fine summer's day an endless crocodile of walkers will pace up and down the paths of its southern shore, while lurking fishermen vie for pike. On an early morning in January, however, the paths, the lake and even the carpark were all deserted as I squeezed into my wetsuit and set out to discover one of the nicest swimhikes in the Lake District.

The swimhike begins at the Rothay ford above the lake. Wading in, the river shelves quite steeply and you are soon swimming down the River Rothay, alert for the occasional snag, until the river shallows and empties into the lake. Swim for Heron Island, land just to the south of the rock outcrop and make your way through rhododendrons. From Heron Island a few minutes swim takes you to Little Isle, where there is a sheepfold shelter. 'Rocky Island across the narrow, like the fragment of some huge bridge, now over grown with moss & Trees' is Coleridge's description.* Little Isle also has a stone slipway that leads you back to the water and to the pebbled beach of Rydal Water's southern shore.

Climb the path to the two great caves above Rydal Water. The high cave is easy to enter. Looking out from its gaping mouth at the marvellous mountain view you may start to wonder *is it* a cave? Above you the rocks on the roof jut down—looking rather like teeth. Down at your feet, the ground is more like a rough tongue than earth. And the pool—is it really water?

---

* *Notebooks*, Jul-Aug 1800.

Does it not look more like saliva? One day these jaws will snap shut.[*]

From the dragon's mouth you can follow one of the paths that take you directly back to the bridge above the ford, but a more satisfying route is to take in a high point. Climb south to the false summit and then west to the true summit of Loughrigg. Return to the ford via Loughrigg Terrace.

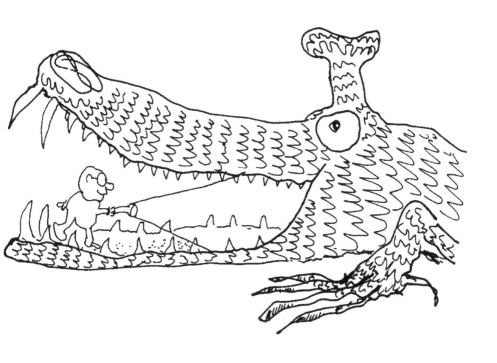

---

[*] Although not quite the same as a dragon, there really are lizards to be found sunning themselves on the walls around Loughrigg.

4. Elterwater

From Elterwater village take the public footpath over the fields towards the lake in preference to the hemmed in 'permissive' path. At the wood enter Great Langdale Beck and wade 150 yards to the edge of Elterwater (the river is only intermittently swimmable). Enter the lake from the spit, a steep descent into deep cold water. Swim to the south east corner where there is a shallow, reedy muddy entrance to the River Brathay—a kind of crawl in both senses of the word will see you through. Swim downriver through a small pool. Exit at a second pool, on a natural beach by the meadow and a couple of trees. (If swimming further watch for waterfalls!)

From the meadow take the path east past Skelwith Force to Skelwith Bridge. Climb the minor road to Tarn Foot, the bridleway to below Ivy Crag and the footpath to the summit of Loughrigg.* Descend directly west by the stream and follow the paths and minor roads back to Elterwater.

---

* Astute readers will be asking: 'Why not swim in Loughrigg Tarn too'? Well, the tarn is slightly cutesy and would be anticlimactic after Elterwater with its dramatic river entry and deep cold water. Also, Loughrigg Tarn is delicate and pond-like; it can certainly sustain a few swimmers, but not too many. But the real reason is that after Elterwater I was feeling too cold to go in again.

The Dragon's Phone Call

Janine: Hello. Can I speak to Peter Hayes please?

Peter: Speaking. Yes. This is He.

Janine: Hi, I'm Janine and I'm calling from the BBC's Dragons' Den

Peter: Oh Yes. Ha ha. I sent in an application a couple of months ago.

Janine: Yes, and it sounded really interesting, have you got a few minutes?

Peter: Sure.

Janine: Tell us a bit about your invention.

Peter: Well, it's a lovely sunny day, it's sunny, and you come to a lake, well, and you think, wow, I'd like to be on the other side, so you swim across it, and you get your things out, because you'd put them in, on the other side, before, and then you get them out and they're dry so you just keep on going.

Janine: I see. It sounds amazing. And could you describe the bag?

Peter: Well, it's just like a normal rucksack really, except it's got a special strapping thing, and a waterproof bag inside.

Janine: I see, and how do the straps work?

Peter: They go below your shoulders and round your waist. So you can swim all the strokes. Even backstroke and butterfly. Yes, I quite often swim *butterfly* with it. And, oh yes, there are these things you blow up, in the pockets, not really for buoyancy, for balance.

Janine: I see, and does the bag weigh you down at all?

Peter: No, I mean, I time myself, I'm not really a very fast swimmer *[subtext: 'I am a fast swimmer']* but when I swim across something, it makes no difference, it's like the bag's not there.

Janine: Does it help?

Peter: It's not meant to help, No. Absolutely not. That is not the point of the bag. No.

Janine: But it's not dangerous? With currents?

Peter: Dangerous? *[deprecating laugh]* Well, currents aren't a problem but wind, you're more exposed to wind, and waves. No. I wouldn't advise people to go in when its windy or wavy. I mean me, I myself, *I* go in in all conditions, Ha ha. But *other* people, No, I wouldn't advise *them* to.

Janine: You've seen the Dragons' Den haven't you?

Peter: *[Thinks: Shall I say "Only idiots watch Telly" ?]* No. But it's on the internet isn't it?

Janine: I expect so. Anyway it's simple, you get a three minute pitch and then they ask you questions.

Peter: Oh well, I can practise for that all right then, When do you want me to come?

Janine: Have you got a business plan?

Peter: Yes *[sort of]*.

Janine: Did you get help with it or do it yourself?

Peter: *[proudly]* I did it all myself.

Janine: How much money do you want?

Peter: £120,000.

Janine: And what equity do you want to give?

Peter: Er, *[sounding cunning]* well you see there is what I would give, and what I would say see? See—they're different. Well, let's say 30%.

Janine: OK 30%. Has anyone else invested any money?

Peter: No. But I'd like someone else too, instead of all my own money.

Janine: How much have you invested?

Peter: *[Thinks: Not very much, better make it sound a bit higher]* £1,500.

Janine: Oh.

Peter: And time, a *lot* of my time.

Janine: What do you want the money for?

Peter: Well, I'd like to improve the bag a bit first.

Janine: So it's not finished yet?

Peter: Well it almost is, There's another strapping system I want to try, and push buckles, and whether to have fabric that's resistant to seawater.

Janine: But you have a prototype?

Peter: Oh yes. Made in China, Not very patriotic I know. Ha ha. Yes, [*importantly*] I've got connections in China.

Janine: What connections?

Peter: Well, I've got friends in Japan, and they go to Shanghai. A lot.

Janine: I see. How much would it cost to make the bag?

Peter: Between 15 and 18 pounds, including transport.

Janine: And how much to sell it?

Peter: £47.50

Janine: And what about to retailers?

Peter: Er. Well, that's the thing see. I hear horrendous stories about how they'd want a big cut. So, well, so I don't know what they would accept.

Janine: And have you been in contact with them yet? [*somehow making it sound like I ought not to have been*]

Peter: No.

Janine: So you haven't contacted Millets and they've said they'll take so many bags?

Peter: No.

Janine: Have you had positive reports for the bag, I mean from people who have tried it?

Peter: Oh yes, all my friends [*I have virtually no friends*]. I have an extensive network of outdoor adventurers, and they all love it. You see, my marketing strategy is to get outdoor people to use it first on adventures. I mean like really amazing things and, I mean, well, I think its silly, but people are impressed by that, by the cachet, and then they'll want to do it too, and then I can sell it to beach users.

Janine: Have you done any market research?

Peter: Not as such, not in the sense of phoning people up, no.

Janine: What about your competitors?

Peter: Well there are Navy Seals bags, but they cost about 700 dollars, and then, for waterproof bags, they aim them at cyclists and snowboarders and stuff.

Janine: Have you got a patent?

Peter: Yes

Janine: What area does it cover?

Peter: Just GB.

Janine: If you've got a patent, you shouldn't have to worry about competitors.

Peter: Ha ha. But I know it's useless, because I worked for someone once, an entrepreneur who made sleeping bags, and lightweight towels. Well, when people copied him, he wrote them a solicitor's letter, and then, if that didn't work, he gave up. So I *know* that my patent's useless. I mean—Ha ha—what am I going to do if Nike copies me? Go to court and argue against their QC?

Janine: What's your background?

Peter: Well, I've been a fell runner for a long time and a swimmer. I started training for the Channel.

Janine: The Channel! Wow!

Peter: Yeah, but I didn't do it. I had a bad experience. I was all covered in lanolin, in sheep's grease, and I got cold, in Wastwater. I'd gone in at the beginning of June, which was too early, and I had to crawl out onto the screes, and I was so cold I almost had hypothermia and if anyone had come I was going to ask to wear their clothes, even though I was covered in sheep's grease, which would have ruined them. But luckily no one did come, and by the time I got back to the campsite I felt all right. So after that, I thought I'd forget about the Channel and just enjoy my swimming. And now that's what I do, with the swimsac.

Janine: I see. And what about your work background?

Peter: Oh, that? I'm a politics lecturer at the University of Sunderland.

Janine: Have you ever been in business for yourself before?

Peter: No, only an employee.

Janine: I'm going to ask you one final question. How committed are you to this project.

Peter: [a long pause] I am very committed.

Janine: Well, thank you Mr Hayes. I don't think that your project is quite advanced enough for the Dragons. You see, they want something that they can invest in straightaway, something that is ready to go, something that has already got retailers saying: 'Yes we will order it'. But I will put it past the production team, and if they like it, I will let you know.

Peter: Oh.

Janine: Thank you and goodbye.

Peter: Goodbye.

Mungrisdale

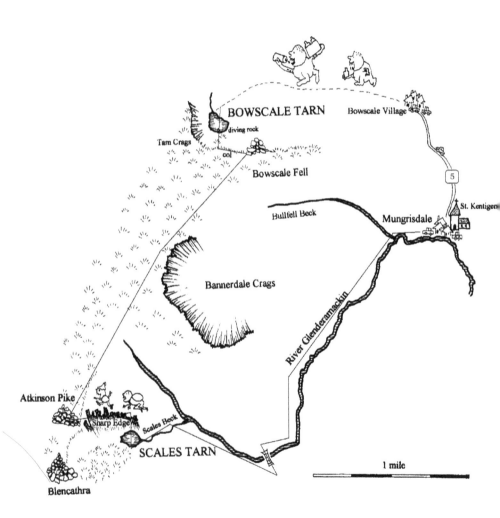

BOWSCALE TARN

Bowscale Village

Tarn Crags

diving rock

col

Bowscale Fell

Bullfell Beck

Mungrisdale

St. Kentigen

5

Bannerdale Crags

River Glenderamackin

Atkinson Pike

Sharp Edge

Scales Beck

SCALES TARN

Blencathra

1 mile

5. Scales Tarn and Bowscale Tarn

Mungrisdale in the North East Lake District, has an old fashioned feel, as though the rush of traffic down the A66 has passed it by and left the village behind in an earlier, slightly gentler age. The several car parks all rely on honesty boxes. A white haired shepherd with a crock passes by taking long strides, and a young farmer herding cows says 'Hello'. (He is, admittedly, astride a motorised buggy.) The hills too are a little softer and rounder than the craggy fells of the central Lake District. So it is slightly surprising that up amongst them is one of the most *exhilarating scrambles* in the Lake District: the knife edge ridge of Sharp Edge above Scales Tarn.

From Mungrisdale follow the path beside the River Glenderamackin past Bullfell Beck before branching off up Scales Beck to reach the lip of Scales Tarn. This beautifully clear round pool is everything you could ask of a tarn, apart from being rather cold. From the centre is an excellent view, the half encircling fells like great waves about to crash down. And once you have reached the middle, you will want to take advantage of the swimsac on your back to keep on swimming to the other side. But should you cross the tarn from north to south or south to north? If you swim from north to south, you can ascend the moderate grass slope to Blencathra before turning back to Atkinson Pike. If you swim south to north, you can head straight up the scree for the *exhilarating scramble* along Sharp Edge.

Frankly, I would advise the grass slope. For myself it is always the same story. I look up. I think: 'That does not look so hard. Anyway, how difficult can it be? Even my wife's climbed it'. Then as I climb optimism turns to terror and I end up crawling along in a state of vertigo-induced near paralysis.

To make things worse, as I tread fearfully along the chicken track on the north side of the Edge, there is invariably someone above me, skipping like a goat from one toothed rock to the next while making cheery comments like 'What *fun* this is'!

Sharp Edge leads directly to Atkinson Pike, and from there a grassy track leads north past Bannerdale Crags towards Bowscale Fell. Looking back you will see the Pike as a mottled green crag, quite distinct from the rolling fells around it. From Bowscale summit the tarn is invisible, but north of the col, the blue water appears below Tarn Crags. A direct and steep descent brings you out at the flat platformed diving rock. Dive in—a swimsac can cope with a shallow dive--and swim across the centre to the northern shore. Avoid the northwest corner which is too shallow for swimming.

Bowscale Tarn is not quite as clear as Scales Tarn, but it is warmer and is a most inviting place to swim. But arrive early if you want it to yourself, for a wide and easy bridleway makes for an easy passage up from the road at Bowscale Village. And look! Who is this coming up the other way? Staggering under their heavy loads of tents and throw-away barbecues and six-packs are five sweaty, shaven-headed, tattooed men, each bringing a little piece of Newcastle with him into paradise. No doubt they are all fine fellows once you get to know them, but if you are not inclined to be sociable you had better be up with the lark.

The minor road brings you back to Mungrisdale and the Church of St. Kentigern (or Mungo), on the site where the Saint raised a cross while hiking to Pembrokeshire in the sixth century. The current Georgian church has clear windows on three sides. Behind the altar they frame green fields and hills, a gentle pastoral landscape more beautiful than any stained glass.

In sharp contrast to the dull Herbert of Derwentwater, Saint Kentigern had a life full of adventure. The excitement started even before he was born when his unmarried pregnant mother—protesting all the while that she was a virgin—was cast adrift in a small boat and was rescued by fish. It ended only when Kentigern died of pleasure on experiencing his first hot bath, at the age of 185. (What a marvellous way to go, and what a good innings!) Saint Kentigern walked everywhere, refusing to use a horse. He spent his days climbing mountains and at cockcrow each morning he would jump into the river and sing psalms. He also crossed seemingly impassable rivers on his journeys. Jocelyn of Furness attributes this to God making a passage for him like Moses and the Red Sea.[*] From what we know of Kentigern's character, however, it seems more likely that he simply swam across after putting the holybook that he always carried with him in some primitive form of swimsac. Saint Kentigern, in other words, was a swimhiker.

---

[*] *The Life of Kentigern*

The Centre of a Lake

The exact centre of a lake, like the top of a mountain with its multiple tops, cairns and pikes, can be difficult to pinpoint. To confuse things, the surface of a lake actually has two centres, an area-centre and a volume-centre. The area-centre of the lake is the point with an equal area of water on all sides. This is easy to identify if the lake is more or less round, like Scales Tarn, but more difficult if the lake is a funny shape.

To find the area-centre of a lake: (1) Cut out a piece of paper in the shape of the lake, and (2) Try and balance it on the blunt end of a pen. The point where the paper balances is the centre.

The area centre of the lake provides, on average, the best panoramic view. Your angle of vision is unimpeded on all sides by the flat water around you, so that behind the immediate hills, higher but more distant mountains come into view. By contrast, when a mountain summit is somewhere in the middle of a tabletop plateau, as many tops are, the flattish area immediately around you has the opposite effect of restricting your view by blocking what is below you from your sight. So it is, that the view from the centre of a lake is often better than the view from the top of a mountain.

The volume-centre of the lake is the place on the surface with an equal volume of water on all sides. If one side of a lake is too shallow for swimming, like in Bowscale Tarn, then it may be more natural to swim across the volume-centre, which will be closer to the middle of the deeper water.

To find the volume centre of a lake: (1) Cut off a hunk of bread with a sharp knife—the cut edge represents the surface of the lake. (2) Gnaw the sides of the bread into the shape of the lake on the surface and nibble the uncut underside of the bread into the shape of the lake underwater. (3) Try and balance the flat end of the bread on the top of the knife handle. Where the bread balances is the centre.

Alternatively, you can just guess.

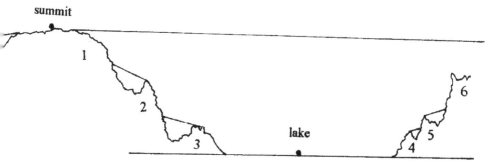

Six mountains are visible from the centre of the lake, but none are visible when looking toward the lake from the flat topped summit.

Lakes around High Street

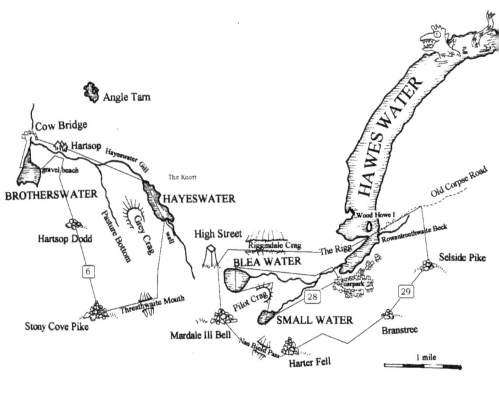

Angle Tarn

Cow Bridge

Hartsop Hayeswater Gill

The Knott

gravel/beach

BROTHERSWATER

HAYESWATER

Grey Crag

wall

High Street

Hartsop Dodd

Pasture Bottom

Riggindale Crag

BLEA WATER

6

HAWES WATER

Wood Howe I

The Rigg

Rowantreethwaite Beck

Old Corpse Road

Selside Pike

carpark

28

29

Pilot Crag

Threshthwaite Mouth

SMALL WATER

Stony Cove Pike

Mardale Ill Bell

Nan Bield Pass

Branstree

Harter Fell

1 mile

6. Hayeswater and Brotherswater

Many years ago, as carefree teenagers, my brother John and I took a tent and went wandering round the Lake District, 'bagging' tarns along the way by swimming across them. (This was before the invention of the swimsac, so we then either had to swim back again or to pick our way round the edge in our bathing trucks.) One day we happened across Hayeswater. We were delighted to discover that its name on the map was our own surname, so we ran down and bagged it. What next? John looked at the map and got tremendously excited.

'Hey Pete, this is amazing! There's another lake just down the hill and, it's called Brotherswater! *Brothers*water! Like us! *We're* brothers! Let's go and bag that one too'.

I looked at the map. It was tempting. But then, what's in a name? So what if the lake was called Brotherswater? It was down in the valley and I wanted to stay high, as far away as possible from civilisation, and not have the walk ruled by silly coincidences. And there was another tarn nearby, Angle Tarn, that I thought looked better. I persuaded my brother that we should head there instead.

I have always regretted this decision. When we reached Angle Tarn it was reedy and shallow and no good for swimming at all, while if we had followed John's intuition that as brothers called Hayes who had just swam in Hayeswater it was natural and obvious that we should next swim in Brotherswater, we would have discovered that that swimming conditions were excellent. This swimhike makes amends for that mistake.

The route connects three points: Cow Bridge—a nice old humpbacked bridge in the valley, Stony Cove Pike, and the Centre of Hayeswater. Without doglegs, and without being overly circuitous, the natural line from the bridge to the summit is to follow the path down the west bank of Brotherswater and swim directly across to the gravel beach at the northeast corner. The first quarter of the crossing has clinging reeds, so keep your legs high; the water is bitty but pleasant. Cross the road and take the footpath toward Pasture Bottom before branching off for Hartsop Dodd, and Stony Cove Pike. Cross Thresthwaite Mouth, climb to the dip in the ridge to Grey Crag and run down the steep grass slope. Part way down you will find a sheep trail that descends gently down the upper Hayeswater valley to the lake. A doe and faun, its coat flecked with white spots, crouch together as I pass by early one July.

A long wall now underwater but still visible marks the start of the swim down the length of Hayeswater. The lake is shallow at first and then deepens as you swim. Emerge just east of the dam wall. (For a shorter swim you can go west to east across the middle and take the gulley up The Knott before descending.) Follow the track down past the superb picnic spots and pools of Hayeswater Gill. At Hartsop village, follow the short stretch of road back to Cow Bridge.

Wild Camping

There is something magical about wild camping. House prices depend on 'location, location, location', and hotels charge extra for a room with a view. But the nicest of locations and the very best views are free. A wild campsite is centred on more spectacular natural beauty than any building because *there are no buildings*. It gives unsurpassed views of the countryside by day, and if it is far enough away from the glare of civilisation, it will reveal a night sky to astound the city dweller. An unexpected bonus is the food which, provided only that it is hot, will taste better than the cuisine of the finest restaurant. A freeze-dried package of some type of spaghetti thing will taste absolutely delicious and if you can add some lumps of cheese, or corned beef, or tinned tuna to the mix, you will be in gastronomic heaven. This is odd, because if you cook up the same stuff at home, it is so unpleasant as to be virtually inedible.

The ideal *des res* for a wild campsite is a flat little patch of grass close to a stream, sheltered from the wind but with a clear aspect to the east for the morning sun. Once you have found your site, you simply kick away the sheep dung, pitch your tent and, and …

At this point many if not most wild campers will break in excitedly 'and light a fire'! In the Lake District, where wood is scarce, some will even pack a bundle of faggots in their rucksacks for the purpose. I do not think you should light a fire though. A wild campsite should be left exactly as you found it, and if you light a fire it will leave a dirty black patch on the grass. Use a stove instead.

Seathwaite

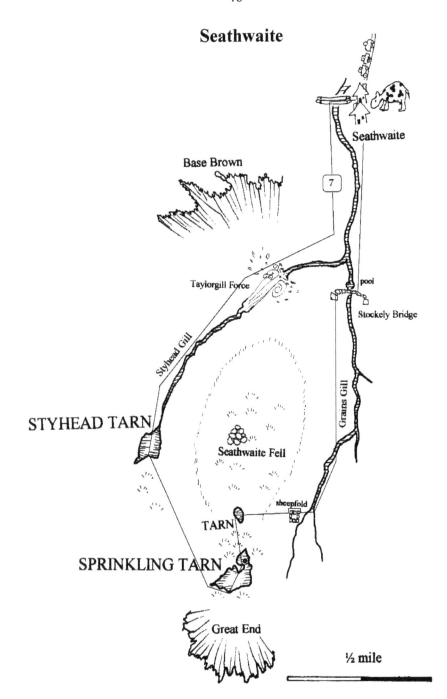

Seathwaite

Base Brown

7

Taylorgill Force

pool

Stockely Bridge

Styhead Gill

Grains Gill

STYHEAD TARN

Seathwaite Fell

sheepfold

TARN

SPRINKLING TARN

Great End

½ mile

7. Sprinkling Tarn and Styhead Tarn

From Seathwaite climb the footway up Grains Gill. You will naturally want to get off this nasty thing as soon as possible, so watch for a sheepfold and cut directly up the steep slope of Seathwaite Fell for the unnamed tarn just above Sprinkling Tarn. Swim across east to west—it is shallow but swimmable. At the far bank you do not need to change, one of the pleasures of this swimhike is to wander barefoot down the grass to Sprinkling Tarn.

Sprinkling Tarn is superb with steeply shelving, deep blue water. Swim to the promontory, climb out and in again to the southern shore beneath Great End.

Descend to the south shore of Styhead Tarn and swim to the north. The tarn is shallow with bright yellow-green reeds beneath the surface, but they do not hinder swimming.

Return to Seathwaite on the path west of Styhead Gill that skirts beneath the cliffs of Base Brown. Part way down Taylorgill Force is spectacular, but so much on this route is spectacular that it barely stands out. This west path is surprisingly tricky, so on a family hike it is better to keep to the footway that runs down the east side of Styhead Gill to Stockely Bridge. Providing the river is not in spate, the pool at the bridge is delightful for swimming.

8. Angle Tarn and Bowfell

The road up the Langdale Valley goes determinedly west as though it will head straight up into the high mountains. Then, at the last moment it has second thoughts and bends away south to climb the col beneath Side Pike. At the bend in the road is Middle Fell Farm, the Old Dungeon Gill Hotel, and a post box. The post box is the starting point for a single high level tarn, Angle Tarn (not to be confused with Angle Tarn near Hayeswater), and the mountain that cradles it, Bowfell.

From the post box take the bridleway up Mickelden Valley and the path—now mostly footway--up Rossett Gill. At the col descend the steep grass spur to Angle Tarn, deep, round and cold. The crags of Bowfell loom above. Swim straight across the tarn and climb up out of the basin to join the path to Ore Gap with its orange stones. Climb to the summit of Bowfell, a jagged rock with a tiny cairn perched precariously on another rock nearby. Why is the cairn so small for one of the highest mountains in the Lake District? Perhaps it is blown away by the howling wind, but sometimes while the wind whips around its flanks, the summit itself can be strangely still.

Descend down The Band to Stool End Farm and take the farm track back to the post box.

Langdale

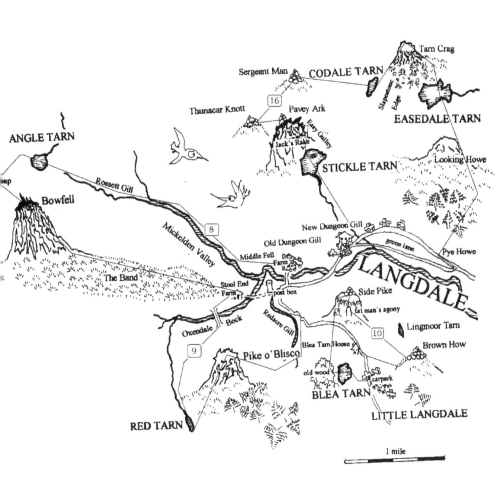

ANGLE TARN

Bowfell

Rossett Gill

Mickelden Valley

8

The Band

Stool End Farm

Oxendale

Beck

9

Middle Fell Farm

post box

Redacre Gill

Pike o' Blisco

RED TARN

Sergeant Man

CODALE TARN

Tarn Crag

Slapestone Edge

16

Thunacar Knott

Pavey Ark

EASEDALE TARN

Easy Gully

Jack's Rake

STICKLE TARN

Looking Howe

New Dungeon Gill

Old Dungeon Gill

green lane

Pye Howe

LANGDALE

Side Pike

fat man's agony

Lingmoor Tarn

10

Blea Tarn House

Brown How

old wood

carpark

BLEA TARN

LITTLE LANGDALE

1 mile

9. Red Tarn and Pike o'Blisco

The post box at the bend in the Langdale Valley provides the starting point for a second, gentler route that also joins a tarn and mountain. Follow the road south towards the pass. Turn off above Red Acre Gill and take the footway up Pike o'Blisco. In some places a natural path runs parallel to the footway, but the footway-builders are crafty at filling alternative paths with rubble or blocking them with stones.

Enjoy the fabulous view from the summit and descend off the path to the southeast corner of Red Tarn where there is a grass and stone entry point. At first it seems barely possible that you can swim in the tarn as much of the edge is surrounded by rushes. Once in the water however, the tarn is entirely clear and it is possible to swim its full length to exit at a low flat rock at the northern end, just west of the outlet. Red Tarn is indeed reddish and is very shallow, only about three foot deep throughout. The tarn follows the heat of the day and cools off or warms up quickly. Early in the morning after a cold night, steam rises from the surface as the heat dissipates.

Descend the path to the footbridge over Oxendale Beck. The last vestiges of natural path have now been destroyed, ('repaired') by a well meaning but dreadfully misguided footway consortium made up of the National Trust, The Heritage Lottery Foundation, The Friends of the Lake District etc.

Follow the path to Stool End Farm and back to the post box.

Paths and Footways

The line of a path is a collective work of art. Countless individual decisions about where to next to put your foot create a work of subtle genius that bends and twists its way across a landscape, sometimes broad, sometimes narrow, splitting and converging. Unpredictable, and yet perfectly in tune with every bump and hollow; the only thing about which you can be certain is that, like the freehand line of an artist, the path made by thousands of free feet is never quite straight. What a pleasure it is to walk these paths, to become a part of them, to help, in a tiny way, to create the line and maintain it against the continual gentle push of vegetation that would cover it over. The feel of the land through the soles of your shoes, the lie of every stone, even the wet and the mud allow you to experience more deeply the soil on which you walk.

Occasionally, very occasionally, a natural path gets out of hand; too much river water joins it, it erodes too quickly, becomes too wide. Something needs to be done, and one solution it to impose an artificial footway on the affected area. The footway destroys the natural path. It is planned not created spontaneously. It cuts the connection between the foot of the walker and the land on which they walk, for a stone footway is singularly unpleasant to walk on. It appropriates the natural line of the path as an evolving living thing and kills it stone dead. The powerful bony line of the footway is the skeleton of a dead path; the immovable pitched stones are the backbone, the leets are the ribs.

To kill a path in this way is—or should be—acknowledged as an act of desperation, a last resort, something to be done with a heavy heart. But in a dreadful mistake the destruction of natural paths and their replacement by footways has snowballed. Footways proliferate indiscriminately, their supporters display a crusading enthusiasm for more and more and will not rest until the last path has been killed. It is not just badly eroded paths that are destroyed; *all* paths are eroded, *all* paths must be replaced by footways. Even where there are no paths, or no paths to speak of, footways are springing up. Stone footways are being built across bogs so that people do not get their feet muddy, they are built over rock steps so that people do not need to climb them. The footway makers adopt a moralistic Orwellian language: they are not killing paths they are 'repairing' them. They are not destroying the chance of future generations to enjoy being a part of a natural path, they are 'rescuing' the fells for future generations to enjoy.

I am not sure what lies behind all this. The desire of outdoor goods companies and professional mountaineers to market themselves as 'caring' about the fells by ostentatiously making donations or by lending their names to the projects has undoubtedly played a small part, but it is the revenue from car parking fees and the lottery that has provided an endless supply of funds and has given footway building its unstoppable momentum. Perhaps people who feel they want to *manage* a national park tend to be frustrated when, for the most part, the best thing they can do is simply to ensure that things are left alone; building a footway provides an outlet for this frustration. Perhaps the committee members financing new footway projects feel a desire to create, for footways too are a form of creation, albeit a very ugly one. Somewhere too, lurks the vain desire to make a permanent mark on the mountain, with the footway—like a monstrous piece of graffiti—announcing the presence of the committee that funded it.

It is a bitter irony that while huge resources are being poured in to the destruction of the natural paths of the Lake District, countless footpaths over farm land in England and Wales are overgrown, cut off by barbed wire fences, guarded by ferocious dogs and generally made impassable by property owners. Here is a real Herculean task to tackle, a problem that any committee could be justly proud to solve. And yet, on the whole, almost nothing is done about it.

What, if anything can be done about the footways? At first I thought that every time I went up a footway, I might remove one stone. But this is easier said than done: the footways have been built to last a thousand years, and with tears of anger and sore feet I have given up trying to dislodge the rocks. You can try not to follow the footway, but because it has stolen the natural line and because the footway-makers go to some pains to make the area on each side of the footway impassable, this is not easy to do. It is, at least, possible to bear testimony to the destruction that has been wrought. As the memories fade of the beautiful old paths that have been ruined, a new generation will be brought up to believe the propaganda of the footway builders; that they have 'mended' the paths, that all paths were badly eroded. This is not true. A priceless heritage has been lost.

When people have finally come to their senses, perhaps the best solution will be to disassemble the footways and place the stones back on the hillsides from which they were torn. But this will be expensive. Will the car parks still be there to fund the work? For by the time people realise the awful mistake that has been made, the age of the car may well be over.

10. Blea Tarn near Langdale

The scourge of footways is completely separate from the excellent idea of making more paths suitable for wheel chair users, as has been done at Blea Tarn between Little Langdale and Great Langdale.* This is the first of three blea tarns and one Bleawater, to be visited. Blea means blue, but it also surely means bleak—none of the low lying tarns are called blea. So blea tarn = bleak blue tarn.

Take the path from the nearby carpark towards the tarn. Cut over open ground to meet the tarn half way down its eastern side and swim to the rocky outcrop on the western shore. The northern half of the tarn is reedy and the water is quite cold. Take the path through the old wood and north and then east up Side Pike. To get down from the summit without retracing your steps is a puzzle, wherever you go you seem to end up crag bound; even Wainwright was flummoxed.** But do not despair—there is a winding route down on the southern side. Squeeze through fat man's agony between the crags and you are down!

Join the wall path to Brown How. You may be lured off course down the delightful heather scented path to Lingmoor Tarn. Surely on such a pretty path the tarn will be lovely too? But it is not. Not unless you are a frog.*

---

* A footway resembles an endless series of rough stone steps, a bit like the Great Wall of China, interspersed with stone watercourses. It is entirely unsuitable for wheels. Furthermore, people who have joint problems but who might once have managed to get up and down the fells on the paths, now find footways too painful to descend.

** *The Southern Fells*, Lingmoor Fell.

* a *real* frog.

Take the path from Brown How down to Blea Tarn House and
the road.

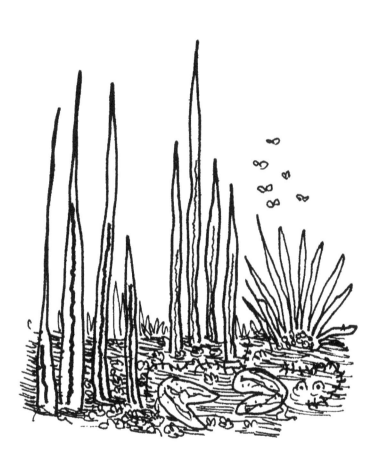

11. Hawes How, Blea Tarn and Harrop Tarn

From the carpark at Dobgill at the southwest end of Thirlmere take the road or lakeshore path north to the rocky point below Rough Crag. Swim to Hawes How Island, keeping well to the west of the two small flat islands frequented by gulls (unmarked on the Ordnance Survey map). The south shore of Hawes How has a gravel beach that extends some way into the wood, Climb the bracken, grass and the well spaced trees to the summit of the escarpment at the eastern end of the island. Retrace your steps, descend to the western shore and swim for the rocky mainland south of the Launchy Gill inlet.

Climb the path on the south side of Launchy Gill, a tremendous rush of brown water when in spate. At the upper fall, the path gives out, but the final climb to the plateau is easy. Scale the fence and cross the pleasant bumpy marshy ground south of Launchy 'Tarn'—a widening of the river. Set your compass to arrive half way along the east shore of Blea Tarn. Swim west over the centre of the tarn, which is excellent for swimming aside from a little surface weed at the inlets on the western shore. Climb the grass bank and follow the natural terrace beneath Low Saddle, cut east to the fence and descend the path to Harrop Tarn.

You may wish to swim *in* Harrop Tarn rather than swimhike *across* it. Most of the tarn is ringed by rushes, lilies and surface weeds, and there is only one natural entry and exit point, the stone spit (that may be submerged) at the Mosshause Gill inlet. It is possible to swimhike to the trees just above the bridge and rapids on the north shore of the Dob Gill outlet, but the way is reedy and the exit is peaty.

Take the north side path down Dob Gill to the carpark.

Lakes around Helvellyn

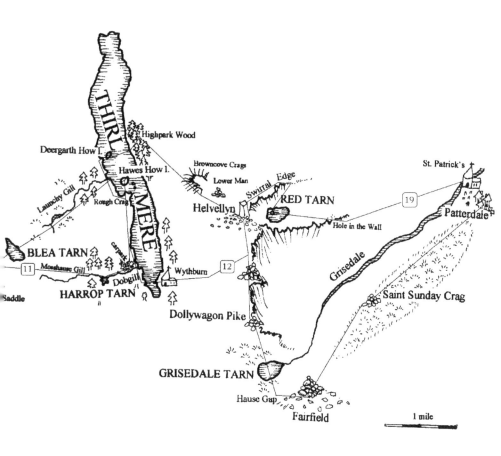

12. Thirlmere and Helvellyn

This triangular swimhike has Helvellyn at its apex and Deergarth How Island and Wythburn Church at the base. From the carpark by the church, cross the road and swim straight across Thirlmere, coming out at a charming section of the shore with grass, copses, stones to sit on and widely spaced large conifers. Follow the lakeshore path north, past Hawes How, until you reach the narrow channel that separates Deergarth How from the mainland. Swim to the island and climb through the birch and evergreen wood to the fern-patch at the summit. Return to the water from the stone slab at the southeast end.

Swim across Thirlmere to join the track to Highpark Wood. Climb Helvellyn. Footways scar much of the ascent, but can be avoided until they start to hog the natural line of the path from Browncove Crags.

Like the centre of a lake or the North Pole, you are never quite sure when you are, officially, at the summit of Helvellyn: there is the trigpoint, the cairn and the shelter to choose from, Perhaps it is best to visit all three.

Descend to Wythburn Church, with its beautiful stained glass set into the alcove behind the altar.

I remember this route for the clouds. In the valley at Wythburn, Thirlmere is invisible. The thick low mist of a grey dawn has merged mere and sky; are those trees shrouded in cloud or are they half sunk in water? It is impossible to tell until a ripple gives the game away. Later near the summit of Helvellyn, wraiths of cloud circle within the corrie at Lower Man and the distant peaks emerge from a sea of cotton wool.

But more prosaically, I should also mention a letter I received from United Utilities, when I suggested that their enlightened attitude towards fishing, non-motorised boating, *paddling*, and *diving* in Thirlmere might be extended to *swimming*.

In a full reply a company manager declined my suggestion on several grounds. He explained that the usual dangers of open water swimming, including low temperature, underwater hazards, the risk of exposure and the difficulties of access and egress, were compounded by additional threats to safety caused by the industrial operations in the reservoir. About fifty million gallons of water were abstracted from Thirlmere each day causing widely fluctuating water levels and unnatural currents. There were bubble mixers on the lake bed to help stratify the water and reduce turbidity and algae blooms. Also, at the dam at the north end, water was drawn off to compensate river levels downstream and there was a spillway where excess water could escape through a rock tunnel.

So there you are. I certainly do not want to make light of any of these risks. As for those readers who are thinking 'Hey! It might actually be rather fun to get tossed around by artificially induced air bubbles', all I can say is that it has never yet happened to me.

The Right to Swim

Look. Let's get one thing straight. I do not trespass on the earth's private parts. And neither should you. A J Wainwright said it best: private property 'must always be respected'.[*] How true! And, needless to add, how scrupulously Wainwright observed this wise maxim in his routes, never once scaling a fence. I think, though, that we can safely go one step further and say: 'Always do what official notices tell you to do'. Or to put it more concisely: 'Always do as you are told'.

OK. Is there a right to swim, and if so, where? To answer these questions we first have to decide which of two concepts of rights we are going to adopt.

(1) The first concept of rights is the positivist idea that *all rights come from the law*. This means that the right to swim (or do anything else) depends entirely upon the law of the state you are in. But this is obviously silly (think of law under the Nazis etc…), and no one seriously believes it apart from a few tyrants and professors of jurisprudence.

(2) The second concept of rights is the idea that *there are at least some rights that exist regardless of what the law says*. Most people take this second much more sensible view.

Is swimming one of the rights that are held regardless of the law? I think it is. As humans we have the right to be free, and a fundamental freedom is the right to move around.[**] Swimming is a primary form of movement for us. We also have the right to experience and enjoy what the world has to

---

[*] *The Outlying Fells*, xii
[**] Thomas Hobbes, *Leviathan*. Ch. 21.

offer. Most of the world's surface is covered in water and swimming through it is an inimitable experience and pleasure.

Where do we have the right to swim? Here a well known philosophical principle can now be invoked: we have the right to do anything that does not harm other people.[*] In the case of swimming, we have the right to swim wherever we are not harming others. As swimming is a particularly harmless pursuit, this means that we have the right to swim almost anywhere. Rivers are like footpaths providing access through cultivated land and lakes are like open countryside, with as much right to swim in Thirlmere as to climb Helvellyn.

Let us now, in a general way, consider objections from people who claim that swimmers are in fact 'harming' them, because they are messing up their fishing, or getting in the way of their jet ski, or spoiling the view.

What is meant by 'harm'? We cannot assume that someone has been harmed just because they *say* they have, or our rights will rapidly disappear. Thus I could claim 'I feel harmed by the mere presence of shaven-headed tattooed men at Lake District tarns: they ruin my aesthetic enjoyment'. Plink!—the right of these men to enjoy the countryside has vanished. To avoid this absurdity, we have to separate (a) being *harmed*, from (b) pretending to be harmed while really being *intolerant, greedy and selfish*, which is not the same thing at all. The notion of harm must be used in its proper sense: a real hurt to someone's physical or mental well being or to their dignity or reasonable enjoyments. Considered objectively, few objections to swimming can be classified as harm in this true sense of the word.

---

[*] Thomas More, *Utopia*.

What of private property? Large landowners like to suggest that 'keep off my mountain' is just like saying 'keep out of my garden', and presumably they think that 'keep out of my lake' is like 'keep out of my paddling pool'. In fact, keeping other people out of small areas of property, which is animated by the need for privacy, is quite different from keeping people out of large ones, which is animated by greed. We all have a right to privacy and everyone can lay claim to a modest area of space they can call their own, a house, a garden, a paddling pool. Privacy allows for intimacy, sanctuary, a retreat from the world, a place for a family to dwell in peace. When private property takes this form it should be respected, and it is quite wrong to intrude uninvited. But what of property that does not retreat inwards but expands outwards, grasping more and more of the surface of the earth? That kind of property goes beyond the bounds of what is reasonably private and encroaches on what should be *shared* property. Owners of a lake or a mountain, must learn to share with other people who observe their duty to treat the earth gently; who could object to a notice that said: 'walkers and swimmers welcome, but please leave no litter'? The more typical notice, 'Private property: keep out' makes a terminological mistake. The notice should really read, 'I am greedy: keep out'.

Does a lake that has been created (or more often extended) by a dam make a difference to the right to swim, because it is 'artificial'? No. You can no more legitimately close off a lake by building a dam wall to extend it than you can close a mountain by throwing a fence around it to enclose it. The test of whether an area of the earth is rightly shared is based on the size of the area, not on whether the character of the surface has been changed by human hands.

'I don't want you polluting my drinking water by swimming in it, thank you. I've seen what your bathwater looks like after you've been in it'! This argument has some force for a very small reservoir, but as the reservoir grows in size, the addition of a few swimmers to the mix of dead sheep, seagulls, car exhaust particles and angling detritus becomes infinitesimal. The prospect of drinking someone else's bathwater is admittedly unsavoury. But a lake is not a bath (for example, the capacity of Haweswater is 85 million cubic metres of water, which is 1 billion times more water than the 85 litres of an average bath). To reassure yourself on this point: consider all the disgusting bilgewater swilling around in the many boats that ply up and down reservoirs. All that filthy liquid will find its way back into the lake. And yet tap water is clean. Consider too that when the reservoir at Thirlmere runs low, the inhabitants of Manchester drink water that has been sucked out of Windermere or Ullswater instead. This little known fact may be a dreadful shock to Mancunians who have visited the harbours at these lakes, Windermere especially, on summer weekends and noticed that the water—if they can see any water beneath the jostling motorboats and greedy crowds of ducks—is rather dirty. But of course, the water they drink is fine, and on exactly the same principle that the dirty bit is a tiny fraction of the whole.

13. Floutern Tarn

From Maggie's Bridge, an undistinguished thing, take the bridleway through High Nook Farm, above the shoulder of Black Crag and along the pleasant terrace above White Oak Beck. Do not be diverted by the Siren charms of the unnamed tarn below Black Crag. It may look swimmable, but it is not, not unless you want to bathe your stomach in peaty mud.

The bridleway peters out in Whiteoak Moss. Skirt west to the summit of Floutern Cop and descend to the western end of the narrow tarn. There are a few reeds here but these are easily avoided. A pleasant swim down the length of Floutern Tarn's peat red water brings you out on large stones at the eastern end.

Climb Hen Comb, descend north down the ridge before cutting down to Mosedale Beck where it meets the wall. Join the Bridleway to Loweswater village.

On the road at nearby Rannerdale is a quaint handwritten sign much beloved by tourists that says:

Take Care
lambs ont road

How lovable Lake District farmers are! Truly the heart of Peter Rabbit Country! But—as anyone who has actually read the Beatrix Potter stories will know—there is a dark side to Peter Rabbit, and on the gate at the bridleway to Loweswater it says:

WORRYING SHEEP IS AN OFFENCE
ALL DOGS CAUGHT WILL BE SHOT

Saint Bartholemew's church in Loweswater is rather big and out of place. The little old church was pulled down and the new one built in 1884 to accommodate an anticipated influx of lead miners. But they never came, and the cavernous building stands empty above the tiny hamlet.

Return by road to Maggie's Bridge.

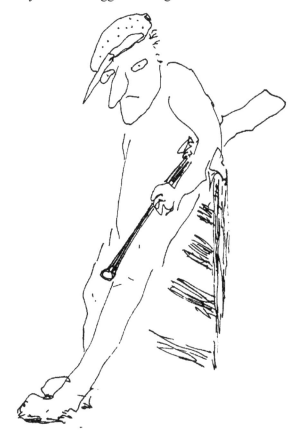

North West Lake District

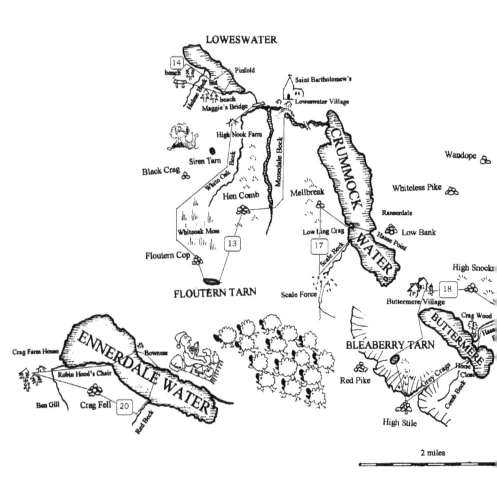

LOWESWATER

14 Pinfold
bench
hut
beach Saint Bartholomew's
Maggie's Bridge Loweswater Village

High Nook Farm

Siren Tarn

Black Crag

Hen Comb Mellbreak

Whitsoak Moss

Floutern Cop 13 Low Ling Crag 17

FLOUTERN TARN Scale Force

CRUMMOCK WATER

Wandope

Whiteless Pike

Rannerdale

Low Bank
Hause Point

Scale Beck

High Snock

18

Buttermere Village

Crag Wood

BUTTERMERE

Crag Farm House ENNERDALE WATER Bowness

BLEABERRY TARN

Robin Hood's Chair

Ben Gill Crag Fell 20 Red Pike

Grey Crags Horse Close

Comb Beck

Red Beck

High Stile

2 miles

14. Loweswater

This little swimhike provides the excuse to swim twice across a lake with a mountain view to the south so spectacular that it rivals the celebrated view east along Wastwater. The Loweswater view is, in a sense, even better, because at Wastwater the view up the valley is so famous and so overused that you will be disconcerted by the nagging sense of having inadvertently swum into the backdrop of an advertisement for some loathsome off-road vehicle.

From Pinfold on the northeast shore of Loweswater swim to the southwest corner of the lake, to the beach where the land meets the woods. Head diagonally up through the trees to Holme Beck and continue northeast on the bridleway to the bench with a marvellous view. Breast the hill then cut down over easy open ground to the wall corner. The wall, unfortunately, is not easy to climb. Once over you can join the footpath to the beach by the hut and swim straight back across the lake where a short stroll down the lakeshore path completes the loop.

National Trust signs warning that the blue green algae in Loweswater may be toxic are festooned everywhere. You are advised: 'Do not bathe, do not let your dog bathe', etc. etc. I swim breaststroke as a precaution, but see no algae. At the beach by the hut, a man watches indulgently as his thirsty dog laps up water from the lake. The signs, he says, are rubbish.

Drowning

Swimming and hiking both pose risks, but there is one obvious difference. If you over-calculate your abilities on a hiking section of a swimhike, you will probably live. If you over-calculate your abilities on a swimming section you will probably drown. This is worth bearing in mind when you are planning your routes.

How might you drown? Being somehow weighed down by the swimsac is, I think, unlikely. Even if the inner bag splits open at the seam and your clothes become sodden the sac still seems to float. For all but the heaviest loads the sac will also float without the inflatables. More likely is succumbing to cold and exhaustion, especially if you have failed to factor in the possibility of bad weather. Swimming into a headwind with waves constantly hitting you can become very tiring. With a swimsac attached to your body you are less flexible in the water and you cannot dive to avoid the waves.

Some drownings seem to come out of the blue, with no prior warning in warm calm water close to shore or the safety of a boat. When I came closest to drowning I was not in the water at all. I had been playing waterpolo and had had the breath knocked out of me and swallowed water in a scrimmage. I surfaced and found I could not breathe, so swam to the side of the swimming pool where I still could not breathe. I climbed out but I still could not breathe, although I was trying silently and desperately to do so. Davey Clark the coach came over and held me and put his hands gently on my chest and told me, calmly, to take little breathes. The warm human contact, the reassuring hands, the advice to take small breaths did the trick and I started taking noisy gasps like the barking of a seal, which everyone had great fun imitating afterwards in the showers. The obvious conclusion for the safety of yourself and others is, like Davey, to take a life saving course.

Wetsuits
A full body wetsuit, with shoes, gloves and a hat, will keep you warm in icy waters. (To help protect your hands you may want to wear wetsuit gloves over washing up gloves.) With a wetsuit strapped to the back of your swimsac or stuffed at the bottom of the outer bag you can go swimhiking all year round. But it drips as you hike, it takes up space, it is a chore to get on and off. When can you leave it behind? As a rough guide there is a long winter season in a full wetsuit, an all too short summer season in swimming trucks, and two little bonus seasons, where you can swim with the help of just a thin wetsuit top and a hat

Winter: September 25-June 15: Full wetsuit
Bonus: June 16-July 9: Thin wetsuit top and hat
Summer: July 10-September 10: Swimsuit.
Bonus: September 11-25: Thin wetsuit top and hat

But people feel the cold differently and what you wear also depends greatly on how far you are going to swim, where, and under what conditions. Consider not only the water temperature, but also the air temperature. You may be able to afford to swim in cold water in just your trunks in hot summer weather where you can rely on warming up afterwards. But what of days—not uncommon in an English summer—when you are freezing cold before you have even set foot in the water? It is also no bad idea to wear a wetsuit in the sea if you are uncertain of the tides or are swimming beneath cliffs with limited opportunities to get out. If you wear a wetsuit unnecessarily the worst that can happen is that you come out of the water feeling a bit sweaty and stuffy rather than refreshed and invigorated. If you do not wear a wetsuit when you need one, you may catch hypothermia or drown. Err on the side of caution.

15. Bassenthwaite Lake

At Peel Wyke you are welcomed by a sign that says you need a permit to enter the lake for 'canoeing, surfing [!], sailing and boating', followed by a phone number. (Thank goodness that it did not mention swimhiking, as I had neglected to bring my phone with me.) Enter Bassenthwaite at the slipway and swim across to Chapel Beck as it floods into the lake like a cold tap into a hot bath. Join the Allerdale Ramble south to the start of Bowness Bay and swim back across the lake to exit on the slippery, artificial and slightly unpleasant stone slope. Watch for Ospreys as you swim back; if you are lucky one might come to take a look at you.

From the western shore of Bassenthwaite you have a route choice. If you are short of time you can head north directly back to Peel Wyke along the depressing straight dark path, shrouded by trees that cut off your view of the lake. You will still be acutely aware, however, that you are next to the A66. Much better is to head south for Beck Wythop and join the C2C cycling trail. Soon after you join the trail a strange sight appears. It is the old main road crumbling away, fading into moss and bushes. Perhaps all Lake District roads will eventually be like this after the oil runs out, or Sellafield explodes.*

---

* The nuclear power station managers had a cunning plan for dealing with the periodic incidents on the site. Every time some radiation leaked out, they simply changed the name so that they could start afresh, rather like a born-again Christian. First the place was called Windscale, then it was called Seascale, now it is called Sellafield. Each name also became more reassuring than the last. Windscale was never a very good name, as it made one think of windborne radiation, Seascale was better, until they irradiated the sea. Sellafield sounds quite cosy aside from the vague allusion to fields concealing concrete cellars of radioactive waste. Now the site is being decommissioned, so

The trail takes you up and out of the woods where a view of the impossibly beautiful Wythop Valley awaits, 'a table of green fields'. Continue to the summit of Sale Fell then take the steep descent to St. Margaret's Wythop or, if you are not interested in lovely churches, take the short cut and join the road 200 yards lower down.

Return to Peel Wyke.

---

we just need to wait a few thousand years for the huge amounts of waste to become safe again. I expect that by the time the thing blows up it will be called something like Mushroom Meadows. It is surely no coincidence that the other nuclear power stations around Britain also have curiously evocative names: Dounreay sounds like Doom Ray; Dungeness evokes the horrifying image of botched genetic experiment on a baroness in a dungeon.

Seagulls

While humanity rushes madly to its doom, seagulls are quietly positioning themselves to take over. They are colonising towns where they already have control of most of the rooftops. They are colonising stretches of moorland, and they are colonising lakes. They are intelligent creatures, and know enough about the technological prowess of their foes to realise that it will not pay to strike too soon. They bide their time, waiting for their moment of destiny.

The first step in a seagull attack is an apparently innocent sound, the same note repeated four times in the rhythmic motif of Beethoven's fifth symphony: 'cluck cluck cluck cluck, cluck cluck cluck cluck, ...'.* You look up, and there, sure enough, is a single seagull circling lazily in the air above you. Then one or two others will glide over and take a look. You are moving closer to 'their' territory. If you are a swimhiker, this is likely to be the lake you are about to swim in (for some reason you are usually safe from their attentions in the sea although young gulls will swoop in to take a look). As you

---

* For it is obvious that the Fifth Symphony is a musical rendition of a seagull attack. Proof of this theory comes from Beethoven himself who was thought to have said of his Fifth Symphony 'That's how destiny (*Schicksal*) knocks at the door'. Can there be any doubt that what he actually said was 'That's how a seagull (*Seemöwe*) knocks at the door'? The famous opening notes of the first movement are the warning cry followed rapidly by an assault. The second movement is a blessed interim when the birds seem to have abandoned the chase. But in opening bars of the third movement they are suddenly back, vengeful and inexorable: cluck cluck cluck Cluck! cluck cluck cluck Cluck! cluck cluck cluck Cluck! cluck cluck cluck Cluck! The final movement is one of bouncy triumph in which the hero somehow overcomes the seagulls. If only this could be so in reality!

get changed into your swimsuit the birds wheel above you; the original tracker is still making the warning cluck, the others are calling to each other. When you enter the water, the seagulls start to scream. Then the attack begins. First there are some steep dives from the front and the sides. Then they fly low over the water straight towards you, intent and ferocious. The worst attacks are from behind. The gull begins its dive silently leaving you unaware that it is bearing down upon you until it is a few feet away, when it lets out a piercing scream. Seagulls only very rarely actually peck anyone, but they are terrifying for all that. And what makes things even worse is that they are, after all, *only seagulls*. You can hardly turn tail and flee. What will you say: 'I was frightened by a seagull'? No, you will just have to plough on.

Sharks, by contrast are easy to deal with. Nobody blames you, and neither do you blame yourself, if you hastily swim back to shore after spotting a shark. But the funny thing is that ten minutes after you have got out, you will probably be back in again. The shark, after all had the chance to eat you, and it did not. And now it has gone, or at least it appears to have gone. Out of sight, out of mind. But seagulls? Even after the attack has ended, the tracker gull still has its eye on you. Listen! 'cluck cluck cluck cluck, cluck cluck cluck cluck, …'. The sound now makes you shiver. You will not lightly enter their territory again.

16. Stickle Tarn, Codale Tarm and Easedale Tarn

Easedale and Codale Tarns are particularly pleasant for swimming, so you may want to limit your swimhike to them, perhaps starting from Grasmere. However, by taking the considerably longer route suggested here, you also get to visit several summits and to savour the delights of Stickle Tarn.

From New Dungeon Gill in the Langdale Valley climb to Stickle Tarn. There is no escaping the footway: there is one on both sides of the gill. The National Trust claim to be redoing them to make them more user friendly, but they appear as unfriendly as ever. Swim across Stickle Tarn to the base of Pavey Ark and climb to its summit.

This may be easier said than done. I took this route in thick mist, and on approaching the tarn heard the warning cry of a seagull. I got changed. Silence. Maybe the wretched bird had gone. I entered the water. I could see less than 50 yards.

'Cluck, cluck, cluck, cluck'. 'Cluck, cluck, cluck, cluck'. The gull had evidently been watching me and had alerted its mate, who immediately starts dive bombing. I feel the air of its beating wings as it comes in from above, from the sides, from ahead, from behind. I keep going into the blank grey mist. They are only seagulls, but I wish I could see *where* I was going. I have horrid visions of swimming round and round being pecked at by them, not knowing which direction to turn for the shore. I pass an island with one small tree. It is no more than twenty yards away but I can barely make it out. I decide not to stop there; the gulls would not be pleased. The attack is unremitting but I swim on and, at last, the bank! I climb out. The gull makes a final swoop. I throw a stone at it and miss.[*]

The gulls are gone, but I am unsure where I am. I try and find my way to Jack's Rake, an *exhilarating scramble* across the face of Pavey Ark, and end up going up Easy Gulley instead.

From the summit of Pavey Ark visit Thunacar Knott and Sergeant Man. Between these two tops you are briefly on the route of the Bob Graham Round. The challenge course links 42 summits in a 72 mile loop from Keswick Moot Hall and must be completed in under 24 hours, if you want to join the club.

At Sergeant Man descend to Codale Tarn. (There is no path and navigation can be tricky. In the mist you may want to join the path to Easedale Tarn and cut across to Codale.) Swim east across Codale Tarn and climb Tarn Crag before descending from the col to Easedale Tarn. Do *not* attempt an apparent shortcut to Easedale Tarn between Slapestone Edge and Tarn Crag; the ground is unremittingly nasty the whole way down. Swim across the centre of the tarn, watching for the pretty little striped fish that flit in an out amongst the reeds. Climb to the east of Looking Howe and descend to Pye Howe back in the Langdale Valley. Take the green lane back to New Dungeon Gill.

---

[*] I returned a year later with my four year old son and swam around hopefully while he sat on the bank with a pile of small stones waiting to throw them at the gulls. The gulls clocked me and swooped in for a look but, to our great disappointment, they were wise to our ruse and did not attack.

The Audition

Tuesday Afternoon

Janine: Hi Peter. This is Janine from Dragons' Den. Can you give me a call?

Tuesday Evening

Peter: Hi Janine.
Janine: We spoke a few months ago and it sounded as if you weren't quite ready. Are you further forward?
Peter: Oh Yes. I've just got back from Japan with a new prototype.
Janine: Great. When can you come for an audition?
Peter: Next week?
Janine: Hmm, that might be a little bit late.

Wednesday Evening

Jenny:[*] No Pete! You idiot! Don't say that. How much are you asking for?
Peter: 120,000.
Jenny: They'll ask: 'Will you give up your job if we offer you this money'?
Peter: No way.
Jenny: Then you're asking for too much. Have you got something to show them?
Peter: Yes.
Jenny: That's good.
Peter: But it doesn't work.
Jenny: Don't tell them that.

Friday Morning

Janine: OK. Look at Philip, not the camera, and give your pitch.

---

[*] My sister Jenny worked in television.

Peter: (*looking at camera*) I'm Peter Hayes. I want £70,000 … (*gives three minute pitch*).

Philip: Three minutes five seconds, spot on!

Janine: So, this is the bag?

Peter: Yes.

Janine: It looks great, and it's waterproof?

Peter: Well, it's meant to be, but actually this one leaks.

Janine: Oh. What about that one?

Peter: That leaks as well.

Janine: Do they all leak?

Peter: Well, the new one doesn't, or only a little bit, where the seam's split.

Janine: So, let's get this straight. You've invented this swimsac, but it doesn't work because it leaks.

Peter: No, No, No. It's not like that at all. It does work. Honest …(*blah*)

Janine: Is it dangerous then?

Peter: No. Not at all. Only if it's windy.

Janine: What about currents?

Peter: Well, currents are dangerous, but they're dangerous anyway. Anyway, I'd write a warning on the packaging: 'Don't swim if it's windy, or if there are currents'. Though actually I do swim in currents. …(*blah*). My view is: if you drown wearing a swimsac, well, it is very sad, of course. But it is not my fault. No more than if you were out walking wearing a rucksack and fell off a cliff.

Janine: But is it though? If you go swimming and get blown away and caught by a current?

Peter: Well, I think if you're an adult and you go swimming and drown, then it's your fault. And the judges agree. I'm not a lawyer, but there was a case where someone drowned, and the relatives complained, and the judge said 'Hard luck'. I know it's a bit macabre but…

Janine: (*breaking in*) So you've got case law on your side. OK, you don't need to tell the dragons that. Has anyone else shown an interest in investing?

Peter: Yes. There was a man last year. But it was all a waste of time in the end. He pulled out.

Janine: Why?

Peter: He was worried about getting sued if somebody drowned.

Janine: What do you think of the opportunity to showcase your idea on TV?

Peter: I don't like it. I'd rather just get the money.

Janine: But the publicity?

Peter: I haven't seen the show, as you know, and actually I don't even have a TV. I don't approve of TV and I imagine that this show is all about embarrassing people and making them look silly.

Janine: That's not the intention I assure you.

Peter: (*trying and failing not to sound sarcastic*) Oh yes, I'm sure that's right and it has a very elevated purpose; educating people about business and things.

Philip: We could send you a DVD of the show if you like. [*]

Peter: Yes please, that would be great. When will you let me know if I've been selected?

Janine: Well, we'll be filming the last slot in about two weeks time, so we'll let you know as soon as we can.

Peter: Good, because, you know, I have other responsibilities.

Janine: Of course, yes, we'll let you know.

Friday Lunch
Jenny: How did it go Pete?

Peter: Really well, I think.

---

[*] This must have got lost in the post.

17. Crummock Water

From Hause Point you can either enter Crummock ¥
the beach or dive in from the north promontory. Loₒₖ ₋₁
the soft brown depths of the lake and you will see beautiful
views of the Central Fells, with the spectacular cliff face of
Fleetwith Pike outshining the higher summits and looking
more like the Wetterhorn than a Lakeland mountain.

Climb out onto Low Ling Crag, a great phallic projection into
the lake, and another place to dive. Climb a pathless route
straight up Mellbreak. The summit knoll has a modest cairn,
nicely understated, and superb views. Descend to Scale
Force, with its wide lower fall and its narrow shoot of water
above that remains hidden from view until you are almost
beneath it, 'a thin broad white ribbon from a stupendous
Height'*. Follow Scale Beck to the lake and swim back to
Hawes Point.

Dinghy Portage

Rubber dinghies have always fascinated me so I was very
excited the first time I went in one, with my two cousins
Patrick and Richard at the Findhorn Estuary. Patrick had used
a dinghy before and knew how to row it, but I was a year older
and felt that it was my prerogative to be in charge, so I seized
the oars, caught a crab, and floundered about as the little boat
became caught up in the current and was carried away from
the shore, round the jetty and out towards the fast white water
where the river meets the sea. As we passed the jetty we
crossed the fishing lines of the anglers and they started to
shout, not because three small children were being sucked out
to sea but because we might scare the fish and tangle their

---

* Coleridge, Notebooks, November 1799

lines. My uncle was there too shouting: 'Give the oars to Patrick'! Frightened, I did, and he somehow rowed us back to shore.

I did not go in a rubber dinghy for a long time after that. There has been, and is, a kind of semi-official policy of discouraging their use in Britain by the prominent reporting, every summer, of all the people who have been swept out to sea in dinghies and drowned. So whenever I suggested that we might get one, my mother always said no, in the same way that she forbad back-garden fireworks in favour of 'safe' organised displays. But when I grew up I started to experiment with rubber dinghy portage in the lakes and lochs of Britain, by tying a dinghy to the back of a rucksack.

You can, if you wish, buy an expensive inflatable canoe. But I would recommend a cheap, low tech dinghy of the kind marketed to children and found in newsagents shops at seaside resorts. This has the advantage of being light, and because it is cheap you will not care overmuch when it tears, as it inevitably will. It is slower than a canoe, but what is the hurry? Tie up the dinghy and strap it, deflated, to the back of a rucksack. Also tie on a single strong paddle purchased separately from a specialist canoe shop and cut to size. Do not try and use the pair of flimsy paddles that come with the dinghy, they will soon break, probably in the middle of a large lake. Take a foot pump and patch repair kit too. On reaching a navigable river or lake, inflate the dinghy, put the rucksack on the floor between your legs and start paddling, alternating strokes on each side.

Portaging a child's dinghy is a good way to cross water when the distances involved are unfeasible for swimming, or where the rivers are too shallow, or where you are camping along the way, as you can use the dinghy to transport a very large rucksack. Still, carrying a dinghy around with you is not everyone's cup of tea, and perhaps this is why about 80% of the people I meet in the mountains laugh, once I have gone past. It must be admitted that there is a bit of a palaver involved in inflating the dinghy at one end of a lake and then deflating it and tying it to the rucksack again at the other. The dinghy is in danger of tearing on stones, snags and broken bottles and it becomes hazardous to use in windy, wavy conditions. Furthermore, the dinghy instructions always say something along the lines of 'only to be used at the shallow end of swimming pools' and while this is mainly a legal get-our clause, it does indicate that the equipment to which you are entrusting yourself and your rucksack is neither particularly robust nor stable.

A Lake District portage route begins at the Portinscale footbridge to Keswick. Paddle down the River Derwent to Bassenthwaite Lake. Paddle west across the lake and make your way to Hause Point at Crummock Water. Paddle across to Low Ling Crag and take a wide arc to the south end of Derwentwater, where you can paddle the length of the lake back to Portinscale. This will take about three days, although the time will depend greatly on how many mountains you choose to visit along the way.*

---

* *Note to 2nd Edn* A short dinghy portage trip to Marshmallow Island and Lingholm on Derwentwater can be seen on Youtube: PTandN, 'Dinghy Portage swimhike'.

18. Bleaberry Tarn and Buttermere

From Buttermere village take the bridleway to the northwest corner of the lake. Here there is, unfortunately, no alternative but to climb the nasty old footway that snakes its way up to Bleaberry Tarn like the backbone of some enormous dinosaur. Swim southeast across the tarn. It is cold and at first it is shallow with leg-brushing reeds, then suddenly blue and deep. From the south shore of the tarn climb east of the rock buttress aiming to take a direct route to High Stile. After the arthritis-inducing footway it is a great relief that there is now no path at all. The crags above you look rather forbidding and perhaps this is why people do not walk this way. As you climb, however, you will see several easy routes to the summit.

There is a path of sorts to descend Grey Crags, but it is a tricky scramble. Bear to the south side of the ridge, the north side is no easier and much longer. Follow Comb Beck down to Horse Close bulging out into Buttermere. Swim straight across Buttermere to the spit. If you want to take a drink, make sure to do so in the middle of the mere as it is rather goosey around its edges. From the spit take the path through Crag Wood to Hassenshaw Beck. Climb High Snockrigg and join the path that takes you west down to the road back to the village.

The Frog Graham Round

Anyone who creates a new challenge course faces a dilemma. The route really ought to be named after them, so that they can be immortalised down the ages as its founder. But they are, of course, far too modest to call it after themselves, and have to call it something else, hoping that in due course the name will gradually revert to their own or, better, will be solemnly renamed in their honour at a special ceremony. So it was that when Paddy Buckley created the route in Snowdonia that is now universally known as the Paddy Buckley Round he called it some other name ('The Welsh something-or-another') that everyone has now forgotten. So it was that when my fell running friend Alan Yates created a loop of the hills around Sheffield he called it not 'The Alan Yates Round', as in truth it should be called, but rather 'The Fifteen Trigs'.

I too was faced with this dilemma when, with the help of a swimsac and a wetsuit, I ran over eighteen mountains and swam over four lakes in one long day on May 14th, 2005. What could I call it? 'The Lakeland Swimhike'? That sounded rather boring. I decided on 'The Frog Graham Round' in honour of Bob Graham and his classic 1932 Round. At least, I think that I am honouring him. However, my father thinks differently. In his long athletic career as a cyclist, orienteer, fell runner and triathlete my father has completed the Bob Graham Round three times and continues in his old age to make further quixotic attempts to do so again. His view is that I am *dishonouring* Bob Graham, and that the Frog Graham Round, while it might be a relaxing bit of fun, so entirely lacks the qualities of a great route that no one will ever bother with it.

Like the Bob Graham Round, the Frog Graham Round starts and finishes at Keswick Moot Hall, but is otherwise, I have to admit, rather easier. Although it took me twenty-one hours and sixteen minutes to complete, an athlete who made no navigational errors could reasonably aim to do it in under twelve. However, I have decided that to join the Frog Graham Round Club you can take *as long as you like*. You can also choose your own route between the checkpoints (numbered below). These are mostly summits, although there is also a church, two promontories and three islands. Needless to add, it goes against the spirit of the Frog Graham Round to run round the edge of the lakes instead of swimming across them. Although not a hard and fast rule, it is also in keeping with the Frog Graham spirit to be self-supporting and to rely on what you can carry in your swimsac to get you round.

Start: Keswick Moot Hall

1.Skiddaw
2. Bassenthwaite Church

Swim **Bassenthwaite Lake**
(Church Bay to Beck Wythop)

3. Barf
4. Lords Seat
5. Ullister Hill
6. Grisedale Pike
7. Hopegill Head
8. Sand Hill
9. Crag Hill
10. Wandope
11. Whiteless Pike

12. Low Bank (at Rannerdale Knotts)

Swim **Crummock Water**
(Hause Point to):
13. Low Ling Crag

14. Mellbreak (S. summit)
15. Red Pike
16. High Stile

Swim **Buttermere**
17. Horse Close
(to Crag Wood)

18. Robinson
19. Dale Head
20. High Spy
21. Catbells

Swim **Derwent Water**
(Otterbield Bay to)
22. Otterbield Island
23. St Herberts Island
24. Rampsholme Island
(to W. point of Calf Close Bay)

Finish: Keswick Moot Hall

The Frog Graham Round

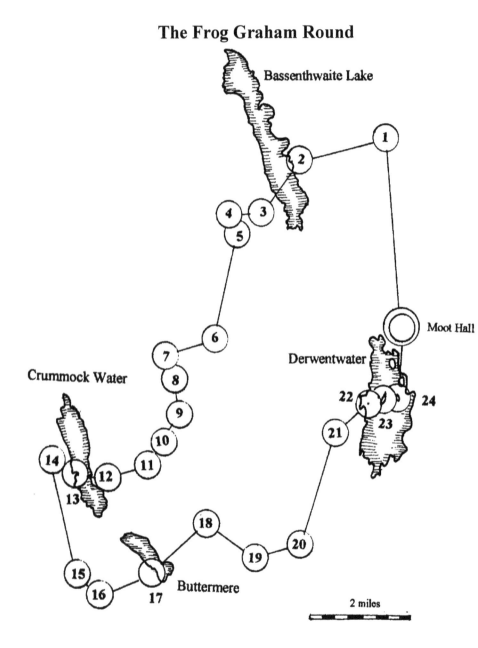

Bassenthwaite Lake

Moot Hall

Derwentwater

Crummock Water

Buttermere

2 miles

The Frog Graham Round made front page news in the Sunderland Echo. The photo shows the North Pier at Roker

The Frog Graham Round Club

As far as I know, the first serious attempt to complete the Frog Graham Round was made by Kate Hampshire in June 2013. Bad weather and a knee injury forced Kate to retire, but not before her support canoe had floated away on its own into Crummock Water *with the car keys*. Kate's husband Nigel Wright swam out to retrieve it, by which time it had capsized. Luckily, the car keys were still there. But this type of thing is always happening to the Hampshire-Wrights.

Later that year, I had an email from Richard Walsh. An accomplished long distance swimmer, Richard told me that ever since he and a friend had found out about the Frog Graham, it had been 'gnawing in their brains', until they felt they had to attempt it. They eventually had a go in October 2015, but stopped part way round. In the meantime, however, Richard had created an excellent Frog Graham Round website and a Facebook page, and as a result, knowledge of the route began to spread.

In June 2014 Tim Mosedale became the first person (other than me) to complete the Frog Graham Round. I have sometimes felt a little anxious about people who attempt the FGR; I had no such worries about Tim. For one thing, he lived in Keswick and was very familiar with the terrain. For another, he had already climbed Mount Everest four times (now six). Obviously, he could take care of himself. Two weeks later Craig Dring completed the Round.

In 2015, Fiona Grove and Ali Mosedale became the first women to complete the Round.

In 2016, Tim did the Frog Graham *again* and Martyn Price, Mike Vogler and Steve Wathall joined the club. By then the route had acquired a sting in the tail: a colony of feisty seagulls had made their home on Rampsholme, the last checkpoint. The gulls have not been welcoming to visitors and several contenders have fallen foul of them. As Martyn put it: 'It might not seem like a big deal, but it's a bit unnerving thinking that you're going to have some big smelly bird bury its beak in the back of your head'.

In 2017, *sixteen* people completed the FGR: Charmian Heaton, Iain Smith-Ward, Jonothan Wright, Thomas Durcan, Kane Tinnion, James Slater, Tom Howe, Paul Wilson, Tom Gomersall, Toby Gomersall, Tom Phillips (fastest man: 13:57), Nigel Wright (who rescued the canoe), Jon Glanfield, Sharon Mcdonald (fastest lady: 16:00), Ian Magee and Stuart Heaviside.

Some of these rounds have been shared endeavours, or ones involving family and friends—and indeed strangers. At Buttermere, Iain *'found a couple (Archie and Cat) on the beach skimming stones who I asked to stay until I got to the other side to check I made it OK'*. (If Iain had *not* made it OK to the other side, I wonder what Archie and Cat were supposed to do about it?) At Crummock Water, Charmian can only secure her wetsuit after she has *'asked a passer-by to zip me up'*. I sympathise with this difficulty. It is hard enough to get into a wetsuit, but worst of all is to find that, having finally got the wretched thing on, that the zip has got snagged at the back. Now what? Well for my part, sometimes I give up and start again, and sometimes I roll around on the beach in a rage.

Another problem on the Frog Graham is getting lost. Jon Glansfield, who managed to get lost almost immediately, gives a fine account of how easily it can happen:

It was all going rather well until I almost found Skiddaw. As I headed up the bridleway the cloud slowly enveloped me and visibility dropped. Somehow I ignored the fact that said bridleway avoided Little Man and crossed a fence line, I also conveniently ignored the fact that my altimeter was reading too low for the cairn I was stood next to, to be Skiddaw, putting it down to atmospheric conditions.

But a nagging and persistent thought meant that it still just felt wrong and looked wrong with 2 cairns. I headed east to see if the fence line was present to confirm that this was Little Man, but didn't see it. I headed back to the summit noting that the fence line north of Skiddaw turned obliquely right, using this as a catching feature I headed north and jubilantly found the turn in the gloom and mist. Determined to make as many navigational errors as I could in as short a timeframe as possible I failed to notice that virtually the same angle was formed by the fence north east of Little Man ... until later. Heading south west off what I later realised was in fact Little Man, I failed to find the path that would eventually lead into Dodd Wood, which was hardly surprising given that it was about 1 kilometre north of my current position.

It must be very faint, a trod maybe, I kidded myself, and blundered on into the fog, losing height rapidly, desperately trying to get what little I could see to match the map. It was about this time that a veil was lifted in the drapes of cloud sprinkling just enough pre-dawn greyness and moonlight to reveal a deep plunging valley, soaring crags ahead and a scree slope, none of which had any right to be there according to my reckoning.

At this point I capped the adrenal glands, slowed right down and took stock. Clearly I had messed up and it wasn't hard to work out why as more light filled the voids around me. I made my way out of what I now acknowledged was Grey Crags and

*back onto Little Man for only the third time, turned north and
finally hit the first checkpoint. It was going to be a long day.*

I know the feeling well. I have a propensity to get lost, and
then to make myself believe I am *not* lost until the very
moment that if I take one more step in the wrong direction I
will fall over a cliff.

Alongside the completed rounds, several people have done
part of the route *before returning safely to civilisation.* In so
doing, they provide the single most valuable lesson to anyone
contemplating the Frog Graham Round: *know when to stop.*

An Eagle

As I am preparing to cross Derwentwater from east to west,
there is a great kafuffle amongst the seagulls at their new
colony on Rampsholme. At first I think merely that they have
spotted me and that, rather like a pre-match rugby team, they
are working themselves up into a lather so that they can attack
me with more vim when I approach 'their' island. Then,
enormous and unmistakable, a golden eagle rises up from
amongst them, and flies almost directly overhead towards
Walla Crag. It is carrying something.

I set out across the lake. It is a beautiful still morning and the
surface of the water is a pure flat mirror of blue. As I swim
past Rampsholme, I steal myself for the attack. But no attack
comes. Instead I see that there are lots of white bits floating
delicately on the water, thousands of them. What are they?
They are feathers; the surface is covered in them as though
someone in the sky has ripped open a cushion and let the
feathers fall. The feathers cover a wide area and are rather
unpleasant to swim through. But the gulls leave me alone.
Perhaps they have had enough excitement for one day.

19. Grisedale Tarn and Red Tarn

This swimhike takes longer than any other numbered route—mainly because of the climbing involved. Red Tarn is also the highest tarn to be visited. The water is cold.

From Patterdale village climb Saint Sunday Crag and Fairfield, then descend via Hause Gap to Grisedale Tarn. The tarn is ringed by steep sided mountains, so that it is almost like a crater-lake. Swim across the middle and climb the open grassy slope north towards Dollywagon Pike, avoiding the footway. Continue north to the summits of Helvellyn. A few yards north of the trigpoint summit is the rocky descent down Swirral Edge. Once below the rocks, cut down the grass to the small island at the north west end of Red Tarn. This island, just off shore, can be reached by stepping stones. Swim east across Red Tarn and continue east to the Hole in the Wall. Descend into Grisedale.

Return to Patterdale following the line of massive and ancient trees that border the road, playing field and graveyard of St. Patrick's Church. There are oaks, one bearing a cape of feathery ferns, chestnut, redwood, and finally yew. The church has a high roof, stained glass windows and—gilding the lily—piped classical music.

Friends and Relatives
After I had invented the swimsac I went through a phase of excitedly phoning up friends and relatives and inviting them to share my swimhiking adventures.

Conversation with A—.
A—: Hello Pete, thanks for the message. I'm just back from the Borrowdale fell race (*blah*).
Peter: How wonderful. Anyway A--, do you want to give the swimsac a go when I come down to Sheffield one weekend?
A—: I'd love to yes! Which weekend are you coming?
Peter: This weekend.
A—: Ah, no. This weekend is taken I'm afraid. My better half, after the Borrowdale you see, I promised... In fact, now I come to think of it every weekend, every weekend for the rest of the summer is taken. But do give me a call when you're here.
Peter: OK. I thought perhaps Ladybower...
A—: Yes. Yes! Excellent idea. It's my fingers you see.
Peter: Oh. Do they go a kind of yellow?
A—: Yes: dead man's finger. It's to do with my circulation. And then, afterwards, it spreads to the rest of my body and makes me feel depressed. But do give me a call when you're down.
Peter: Yes, I will.

Conversation with Mike Hayes
Mike: Mike Hayes speaking.
Peter: Hello Dad. It's me. Peter. Your son.
Mike: Ah! Peter. How are you?

Peter: Fine. Do you want to have a go with the swimsac up in the Lake District?

Mike: Yes! Oh Yes! I'd love to get into the Lakes.

Peter: Well when do you want to meet up then?

Mike: Ah. Well, I'm training for the International Fell Running Veteran's Championship you see. Do you want to do that?

Peter: No. Didn't you say you wanted to swim the length of Wastwater?

Mike: Oh yes I do. First I want to swim down the lake, then I want to get on my bike and cycle to (*blah blah blah*), and then I want to climb Scafell Pike. Yes.

Peter: Well, it would be good training for that then wouldn't it?

Mike: Yes. Well. The thing is, when I swim in a lake, I like to swim at the *edge* of the lake.

Peter: Why not go across the middle?

Mike: I don't know. I just seem to prefer it at the edge.

Peter: But that's the point of the swimsac: swimming across the middle from one side to the other.

Mike: Ye-s. Well, I'll let you know. Your mother wants to talk to you.

Peter: But Dad…

Mary: Peter! When are you going to clean your stuff out of our attic?

Tarn Hows

As long as the English maintain their attitude that open water swimming is cold and dangerous and fit only for their pet dogs, then there is no harm, I am sure, in enjoying a quiet swimhike in Tarn Hows. But what if swimhiking takes off? What if millions of people wake up to what they have been missing and start systematically completing every numbered route in this book? I am not sure then that Tarn Hows could sustain the pressure. The water lilies in particular might be vulnerable. So, delightful though it is, Tarn Hows is not numbered as a route.

Tarn Hows is really more like a very large pond than a tarn. In the summer it is almost bath-warm, and a thick vapour rises from the lake into the cool air of the early morning. If you visit at this hour, do not swim south to north else you will be blinded by the sun and mist, and a magical experience will merely become exasperating as you squint and bump amongst the lilies.

Why a Guidebook?

Why write a guidebook to swimhiking? Is it not enough to say:

Here is a swimsac (or at least, here's how to make one). Now buy a map!

After struggling with this question, I have come up with three justifications for a guide.

The first justification is that a guide helps readers to re-see the world with a swimsac in mind. It shows practical examples of the aesthetic, natural, satisfying and 'obvious' routes a swimhiker can take through the countryside. Swimhiking routes are not variations on other routes, they are unprecedented. There are often no paths on the routes they follow, because without a swimsac the paths would seem continually to lead to a dead end at the water's edge.

The second justification is that a guide can discuss not just *where* to enjoy swimhiking but *how*. This may help to avoid the misfortunes that have befallen some of the other outdoor pursuits which have exploded in popularity. Surfing is the worst example. Surfing was once a low key and entirely wholesome family activity. Then marketers created a fabulous and almost wholly inaccurate picture of surfing in California. (The supposedly 'laid back dudes' of this state are actually intensely territorial and have done their utmost to extend their nation's obsession with private property to the sea.) Aspirant surfers in other countries believed this rubbish and in an effort to be 'cool', perfected the art of being sullen. The perverse image of surfing was encouraged by a leach-like advertising campaign as the purveyors of anti-social commodities seized on the sport to promote their wares. In Japan cigarette manufacturers suggested that every surfer sucked a fag. In the UK, off road vehicle manufacturers suggested that every surfer parked one of their contraptions on the beach. What an awful denouement if swimhiking were to share this fate!

The third and most important justification for the guide is my own self-aggrandisement. To do something new in an established outdoor activity is very hard. If you are a climber, for example, only the most inaccessible and difficult peaks are yet to be reached. But because swimhiking is new, every route, considered as a whole, is a 'first', even though it is easy. So I have done all these firsts! And I want to boast about it.

Imagine that the Lake District lay untouched in another dimension and only I had the magic key to enter it. I would scale a virgin summit—say Great Gable—and call it Great Hayes. I would pioneer the classic route up Hayes's Edge to Hayesvellyn. Then, after I had thoroughly explored the place, and proved it by writing a guidebook, I would magnanimously share the key with everyone else, so that whenever anyone went up a mountain, I would chuckle to myself and think: 'Yes, it was *me* who discovered that route'.

I really am in this position. The Lake District—and in fact the whole world—is open to me in a way that it not is open to anyone else, and the key is the swimsac.

20. Ennerdale Water

From the carpark at Bowness on the north side of the lake, take the track east to the waters edge. Swim straight across for Red Beck. Climb the steep slope beside the beck, then cross the fence and head for the summit of Crag Fell. The Crag is precipitous; be careful in the mist.

Descend west following the line of the Crag. Cross Ben Gill, and continue west down through the wood. At the base of the hill turn due east on the path that goes above Crag Farm House to the point at Robin Hood's Chair.

Question. Why would Robin Hood have sat on the point half way down the lake beneath a cliff?
Answer. When the enemy approached on one side, he could swim across to the other, his possessions safe in a trusty swimsac of some kind.[*]

Swim for the cottage at Bowness. Exit on the gravel beach to join the path past the cottage and back to the carpark.

---

[*] Robin Hood is mistakenly supposed to have lived under a tree near Nottingham, but although he roamed far and wide he was actually based in the hills to the west of Sheffield. He was known as Robert of Loxley—the Loxley valley flows into Sheffield. He lived in a cave on Stanage Edge that lies between Sheffield and Hathersage. His friend Little John is buried in Hathersage Churchyard.

Tourist Sites

The Towns
Intrepid backpackers will feel repulsed by these places, crowded with tourists waddling about in gleaming walking boots. They will want to get in, buy provisions, and get out again as quickly as possible, so that the only information of any use is 'where is the supermarket'? At Keswick there is Booths and a Co-op; at Ambleside there is a Co-op. Grasmere and Coniston both have a Spar. You will find them all easily enough. Most of the villages have a shop. Wasdale campsite has a shop that is only open from 8-9am.

But wait backpackers! There are two further bits of information you need.

(1) Buy plum bread.
(2) In Grasmere buy Sarah Nelson's Gingerbread.

The backpackers hurry away munching their supplies and I am left looking wistfully after them. If only all that I had to lug around was a large swimsac and not a small family! But I do have a family (I am happy to say), and they quite like all the touristy stuff, so I will share what I have found out, starting with:

Attractions for Children

Keswick
The swimming pool is ideal for children to have fun in and hopeless for 'proper' swimming—but with Derwentwater so close, who in their right mind would want to swim up and down in a pool anyway?

On a wet day in August you will wake up, look out of the window/tent/cave and say 'Crikey! Tipping with rain again! Hey Kids, I've got a great idea: let's go to the pool!'. *So will everyone else in the Lake District.* And when you get there, there will be a two hour queue to get in. So bring waterproofs and walk up Latrigg instead. Or, if that is too energetic, walk 200 yards down the road to:

The town museum. This is rather charming, and can keep you entertained in the rain for at least half an hour. Musicians can pick out tunes on a xylophone made of slates off Skiddaw. Outside the museum, if it stops raining, is:

Fitz Park, with an excellent children's playground and pleasant landscaping.

At *Hope Park* at the other end of town you can play crazy golf (dignified by the name 'obstacle golf'), if not crowded out by middle aged men taking the game rather seriously.

Derwentwater at *Crow Park* and next to the main Lakeshore carpark is a good place to laze about with children.

Ambleside
Rothay Park is pleasant and has an excellent playground.

Patterdale
has a forlorn roundabout in the corner of the playing field

Windermere-Bowness
Travel back and forth the between Windermere and Bowness with an all day ticket for a *Pretend Train* (a kind of golf cart

affair) and, better, a real old *Steam Bus* run by amiable enthusiasts.

Peter Rabbit shops are everywhere, but Windermere also has the *Peter Rabbit Experience* (at least it is called something like that), with large models in vignettes from the Beatrix Potter stories. This is a great favourite with the family, who insist on going there at least once every year and often twice.

Scenic Railways

At the south end of Windermere there is an enormous carpark for a scenic railway and for passenger boat rides. The train chugs downstream past one or two interesting stretches of river to deposit you at a station with a tearoom, picnic area and engine shed. The shed is home to slightly sullen train-guys, but they will converse if prodded.

Another train runs to and fro from Eskdale to Ravensglass. A pleasant hike over Muncaster Fell is possible if you can negotiate a one way trip, or you can dump the family at Dalegarth Station and set off for Burnmoor Tarn on a swimhike. There is not much in Ravenglass on arrival apart from an uninvitingly muddy tidal flat. It is as though the village does not quite know what to do with all the people deposited there, and they do not know either, but just wander up and down the road vainly seeking teahouses and Peter Rabbit shops.

Zoos

At Dalton in Furness is the *South Lakeland Wild Animal Park** which, while not actually in the Lake District, is a real zoo

---

* *Note to 2nd Edn* The park has now been renamed the South Lakes Safari Zoo after a number of *unfortunate incidents*.

where you can wander freely amongst emus, lemurs and wallabies in a large enclosure, However, the other animals are given so much space that the human visitors are rather squashed and in the summer it is jammed solid.

I much prefer *Ostrich World* at Langwathby. It has incubating ostrich eggs, and if nothing much is going on with them, there is a quite lifelike display of stuffed baby ostriches. There are toy diggers for children to ride around in and play equipment. The ostriches themselves are down at the far end and can be fed through long plastic tubes. However, the main attraction is a bad tempered animal that is half zebra and half Shetland pony. There is also a café where you can eat a small portion of ostrich steak.[*]

Attractions for Adults

Adult Peter Rabbit venues
At Hawkshead there is a permanent exhibition of Beatrix Potter's watercolours of Peter Rabbit *et al.* It is exorbitantly priced and cynically designed to capture coachloads of naïve foreign tourists, mainly from Japan. I have never been in, but have waited outside, and the disconsolate view of my wife—in and out in fifteen minutes—is that the pictures are disappointingly small. This serves to emphasise the relative merits of Windermere's Peter Rabbit Experience, where the models are approximately three feet high, and some of them move around a bit.

Beatrix Potter's House in Sawrey is also expensive, but it is quite atmospheric and is conveniently situated on a family swimhike route. Here the problem lies with what to do with

---

[*] *Note to the 2nd Edn* Ostrich World has now shut.

your swimsac while you are looking round. You cannot prop it up outside the house because that will spoil the scene for people who want to photograph the façade. You cannot take it in with you as you might bump things, and a helpful staff member will ask you take it off and leave it in the dining room. The only difficulty with this is that a recently used swimsac, especially one that contains a wetsuit, is liable to leave a small puddle on Beatrix Potter's dining room floor.

Teashops
Teashops are everywhere. Our favourite place, run by two men, is somewhere in Grasmere, but we can never quite remember where and always have to search around for it afresh.

Antiques
There used to be a very good antique shop in Grasmere. But it is now gone.

Markets
Keswick market has now largely squeezed out the old junk stalls where you could pick up some tremendous bargains.[*] However, in defiance of all known health and safety regulations, a parrot at the pet food stall still sits on the arm of its owner and shares his meals of Cornish pasty.

---

[*] We once bought a wonderful old warming pan, intricately etched, for next to nothing, and gave it to my parents as a wedding anniversary present. Later the same day, I was disappointed to see my father encouraging his grandchildren to hit it with a pointed mallet. For some years after that the damaged pan hung forlornly in my parents hallway, but has now disappeared altogether.

21. Windermere and High Sawrey

This swimhike is ideal for a family, and especially a family interested in Peter Rabbit. It is also, ironically, the most risky swimhike in the Lake District. The danger comes not from the water but from the motorised boats making their way through the narrow passages that you will swim. In this area the boaters are meant to observe a maximum speed limit of 6mph. But not all do. The rest of your family will not be in any danger, however, because they will be taking the ferry.

From the natural promontory at Ferry Nab on the eastern shore swim across the lake to the western ferry dock, where the road simply leads into the water. Follow the permissive paths that edge the B road, then take the path over fields and past St. Peter's Church in its lovely setting in a green valley. Another permissive roadside path leads to High Sawrey. Here is Beatrix Potter's House, Hill Top. You may have to wait for a timed entry. There is a pleasant tea room nearby.

From Hill Top avoid the road by following a triangular bridleway route to Far Sawrey. You will go past a very real farm with cows locked in smelly sheds. Take the bridleway from Far Sawrey to Harrow Slack and the permissive path to the lake. Here the party splits in two. Family members walk south back to the ferry. You walk north to Coatlap Point and swim to the southern end of Belle Isle. Squeeze through a single line of trees to follow a path along the eastern side of the island until opposite Cockshott Point. Swim back to the mainland and walk back down the shore to Ferry Nab.

Safely back on the mainland you can wander round the Marina and see the big powerful boats that are now restricted to 10 mph anywhere on Windermere. In imposing this rule, the Lake District National Park Authority faced down a vigorous campaign from people who liked racing around the lake in their machines. Everywhere there were slogans. One was 'Speed Changes You' (but not for the better). Another was 'Keep Windermere alive. Say No to the 10mph limit' (but now the lake is not dead, it is simply more peaceful).

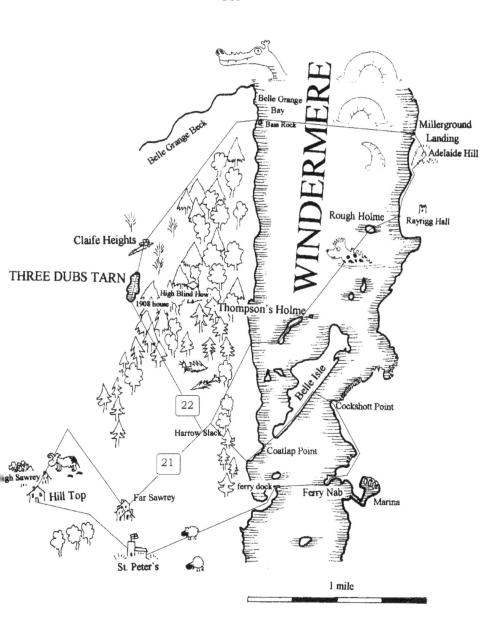

Belle Grange Bay

Bass Rock

Belle Grange Beck

WINDERMERE

Millerground Landing

Adelaide Hill

Claife Heights

Rough Holme

Rayrigg Hall

THREE DUBS TARN

High Blind How

1908 house

Thompson's Holme

Belle Isle

Cockshott Point

22

Harrow Slack

Coatlap Point

21

High Sawrey

Hill Top

Far Sawrey

ferry dock

Ferry Nab

Marina

St. Peter's

1 mile

22. Windermere and Three Dubs Tarn

Rather than hopping across the narrows, this swimhike makes two wide crossings of Windermere. From Millerground Landing climb south up the grassy Adelaide Hill for pleasant views over the lake. Descend south to the shore and make your way towards Rayrigg Hall until blocked by a fence. Swim to Rough Holme. The island has stony ground but somehow trees still grow.*

Swim to Thompson's Holme. This island has two halves. The northern half has soft ground and bushy trees, as well as moss and mushrooms. It is not especially pleasant for walking and you might prefer to swim straight to the eastern beach that marks the start of the southern half of the island. This has a beech wood, firm ground and a path to the southern tip. Swim to the western shore of Windermere. Take the bridleway south past Harrow Slack and then north on the path and forest track to Three Dubs Tarn. Here you can admire the tiny '1908' summerhouse with an arched canoe dock beneath.

Swim the length of the tarn from the dam wall and ascend the summit of Claife Heights, a cairn on a rock ridge. This is the highest point for miles along the western bank of Windermere (although nearby High Blind How has been given the trigpoint). It has a fine view, but the trees are growing fast.

Descend north through trees and rough ground to the footpath and join the bridleway down Belle Grange Beck. From Bass Rock in Belle Grange Bay prepare your swimsac especially carefully for the long unbroken crossing back to Millerground Landing.

---

* *Note to 2nd Edn* Rough Holme now has a treehouse. It is 12 feet off the ground, with no ladder.

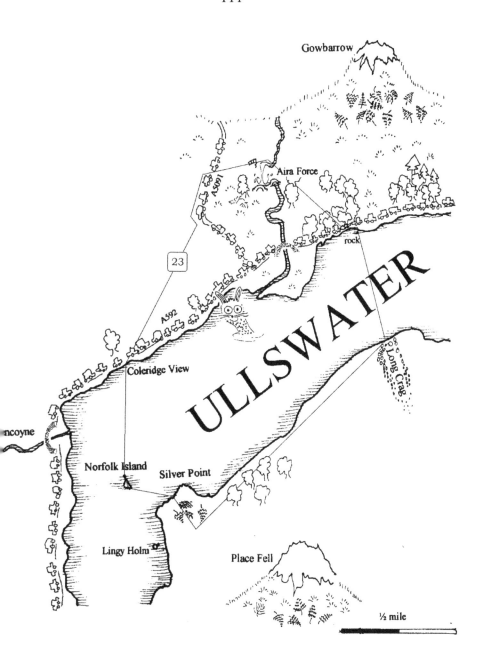

Gowbarrow

Aira Force

A5091

23

A592

rock

ULLSWATER

Long Crag

Coleridge View

ncoyne

Norfolk Island

Silver Point

Lingy Holm

Place Fell

½ mile

23. Ullswater

Much of the northern side of Ullswater is hard by the A592 that skirts its length. In one sense the immediacy of the road is an advantage as there are a number of places between Halfmoon Wood and Glencoyne where you can pull the car over and have a quick dip or family picnic without the inconvenience of having to walk anywhere. The disadvantage is that if you would actually *like* to have a walk by the lake you can't: the road is far too dangerous and unpleasant.* However, the southern side of Ullswater has a lovely lakeshore path, so that is where we will head. And we will avoid the road on the northern shore by starting at Aira Force a little way above the lake.

Most waterfalls in the Lake District have been largely left to their own devices. But Aira Force has been landscaped all around, with lots of little paths and bridges and viewpoints with safety railings. It is all rather pleasant in a tame picturesque way, though one is left feeling vaguely sorry for the waterfall, which has been fenced in a bit like a wolf in a zoo.

Aira Force is ringed with car parks and from one of the eastern ones you can descend to the bend in the A5091 and then take the southerly footpath down over fields and across the lakeshore road to a little beach where a memorable view awaits.

Coleridge arriving here for the first time described the scene:

---

* *Note to 2nd Edn* West of Aira Force things are now much improved by a field path above the road.

I have come suddenly upon Ulswater, running straight on the opposite Bank, till the Place fell, that noble Promontory runs into it, gives it the winding of a majestic River a little below Placefell a large Slice of calm silver—above this a bright ruffledness, or atomic sportiveness—motes in the sun?— Vortices of flies!—how shall I express the Banks waters all fused Silver, that House too its slates rainwet silver in the sun, & its shadows running down in the water like a column—the Woods on the right shadowy with Sunshine, and in front of me the sloping hollow of sunpatched Fields, sloping up into Hills so playful, the playful Hills so going away in snow-streaked savage black mountain—But I have omitted the two island Rocks in the Lake—(& the colors of the Lake all changed! the one scarce visible in the shadow-coloured Slip now bordered by the melted Silver—the other nearer to me, likewise in the glossy shadow, but far removed from the Dazzle & quite conspicuous.[*]

The further island is Lingy Holm and the nearer island is Norfolk Island, half a mile to the south and the next objective of the swimhike. Beyond its rocky shallows this beautiful island can be gained by a sloping stone at its northwest end. There is a tangle of blackberries, flat grass and stone, and one or two trees.

---

[*] Notebooks, November 1799. It is interesting to contrast this passage with the jottings in *my* notebook after I first arrived at the same spot in August 2004: '*The beach is over the fence directly opposite the path's end. The swim to Norfolk Island has the advantage of the view south down Patterdale*'. And that's it. I suppose this helps to explain why Coleridge is a famous poet, and I am not.

Swim east to the crags at Silver Point (from Coleridge we know why so called). Just to the south are rocks mossy and steep, smooth and rounded, with handholds to clamber.

Cut through ferns to the bridleway and take this path north to the rock beach beneath Long Crag. Swim north across Ullswater, aiming just east of the summit of Gowbarrow. The beach on the north shore lies 40 yards east of a low rock. Join the A592 and follow it for fifty yards west. At the first gate cut over a field and wood to join the path back to Aira Force.

The Big Idea Round 1

```
Dear Inventor,

Many thanks for your application. I'd like
to congratulate you and invite you the
Manchester Heats on the 2nd & 3rd September.
We will be in touch via email in the next
day or so to inform you of the times and
location details - but just wanted to
touch base so you can prepare your
pitch…and get excited!
```

The show is hosted at the Orbis centre, and I am so excited that I arrive early. There are lots of telly people milling around--Sky 1, Sky 3, Vodaphone, some internet thing--and all display a gratifying interest in my bag. I have lots of interviews. The sexy lead interviewer tells me that she wants to swim with my swimsac in the nude, and another man is very keen on getting a shot of my bag being flushed down the toilet and coming out with a dry ten pound note. We look down the toilet, it does not look very appealing. Other crew members veto the idea.

OK then, the water fountain.

Emboldened, I point out that this would look silly and offer to swim in the River Irwell, or anywhere else. They would love to, but they have to be in the building all day. Why not just put it outside for half and hour and then it comes in dry? (It is raining heavily.) Well, it would be better to swim in it.

The man wanders off but comes back excited. There is a fountain outside. We can dip the swimsac in the water and then vox pop the young people standing around out there. I look doubtfully at the young people. They are admittedly outdoors in the rain, but they do not look like healthy outdoor types. They are all dressed in black and appear to be members of the 'goth' subculture. The idea is not pressed. Anyway, a young lady interviewer has another idea.

Can you stand outside in your swimming costume in the rain?

She looks at me winsomely and flutters her eyelashes. I politely explain again that I would rather demonstrate the swimsac by swimming.

No matter, the interviewers seem to be interested in my view on all kinds of things. They find out that I do not have a TV. How amazing! Why not? I explain how I think that television is the work of the devil and how watching telly is a kind of living-death. The cameras roll. I must admit that I would have rather liked to have seen this interview on TV. They ask me other questions:

Is there an invention that you wish had never been invented?
Yes.
What?
The jetski.

And I get to explain all about that too. They ask me if I have a special skill, like speaking Swahili.

You mean like a party trick?
Yes.
No.

But some of the other contestants do have party tricks. Julian juggles lemons; Andy talks like Donald Duck.

I try to make friends with some of these other inventors.

Peter: Hello. What's your invention?
Man: (clutching cardboard box tightly to his chest). I'm not going to tell you.
Peter: You're not going to tell me, but you are going to go on telly with it?
Man: If I told you, I'd have to kill you.
Peter: Oh, so it's so good that I'm going to run outside and start making it if you tell me?
Man: I'm working on my pitch.
Peter: OK.

But not everyone is like that, and soon a group of us are sitting around having a laugh.

Julian I has invented a bicycle pump.
Julian II has invented a concave platform that you slide around on while playing video games.

A bricklayer has invented a rubbish sack container
A man in overalls has bought the license to a system for removing condensation from double glazing by inserting a valve.
Richard has invented a bell on a stick
Andy has invented an alarm clock that you can only switch off by getting up and going to the fridge.

We are all middle aged apart from Andy who is a young University of Sunderland student. Bright and personable, with a novel and entertaining idea, I think he might win. We all do. In fact, we start to assume that this is almost a foregone conclusion, and start to gripe that it is unfair Andy winning just because he is young and handsome and has a good idea. If we were young and handsome and had a good idea then *we* might win.

I am called in to the judges first. There is Craig Johnston, former Liverpool footballer and inventor of the Pig Boot ®. There is Ruth Badger, famous for being a runner-up in a TV show. And there is Lord Karan Billacarie who sells beer to Indian restaurants. I give my pitch. Craig likes the idea and Ruth thinks it is OK, so I am through to the next stage, the holding room, where we have to sit and stare at a mobile phone to see it if rings with the news that one of the judges has decided to be our mentor.

I decide to take a walk. The lady at reception says that I have until 4.30. Another TV lady intercepts me.

TV Lady: Where are you going Peter?
Peter: Out. I don't have to go to the holding pen until 4.30.
TV Lady: (sucking her teeth). Better make it 4.00.

In Manchester it is still raining. There are lots of policemen in riot gear on horses. There is a small stand saying 'Troops Out of Iraq'. There is a literary festival where I stand in the rain and listen to an engaging Irish poet recite his work.

I go back. I hang around with the guys. Julian I, Julian II and the bricklayer are all through to the next stage. The man in overalls is gone. So is the man with the box.

At 6.30 we are ushered into the holding room where we sit for another two hours. Andy and Richard are left behind; the judges had still not seen them. Eventually Richard turns up. One of the judges, Craig I think, had liked his bell on a stick.

'What's happened to Andy'? I ask.

'Oh yes. I forgot to tell you. He was turned down'.

A TV person calls for us to be silent and to sit staring at our mobile phones looking tense. This goes on for fifteen minutes with nothing happening. Then Julian I gets a call; Ruth Badger likes his bicycle pump and he is through to the next round. I get a call; Craig Johnston likes my swimsac and I am through too.

24. Coniston Water

The environs of Coniston Water provide a particularly pleasant swimhike that combines a double crossing of the lake with a lovely path on the western bank.

From Dodgson Wood on the eastern shore climb to Low Parkamoor and take the bridleway north, enjoying fine views before you enter the wood. Descend via Lawson Park to Cock Point. Swim straight across to the new pier on the western shore. Just to the north is a crowded, slightly lumpen campsite. A mile or so south, the path diverts away from the lake, cut off by private property. In between, an idyllic no man's land separates the wealthy from the rabble.

Take the lakeshore path south along a delightful rooty trail, with widely spaced trees. Before the path leaves the shore, cut down to the pebble beach and swim back to Dodgson Wood.

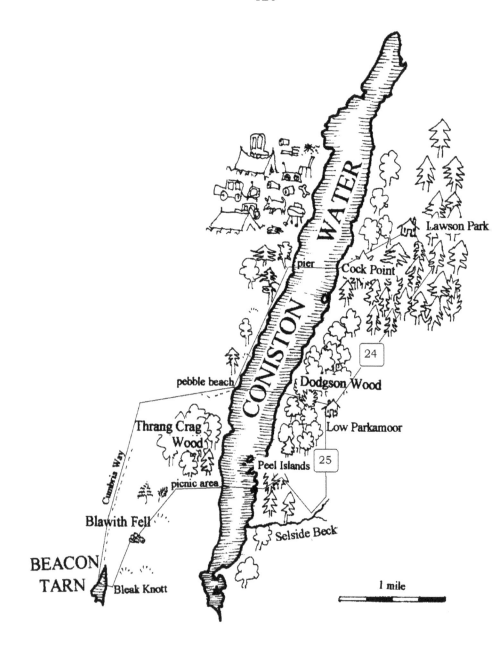

Lawson Park

Cock Point

WATER

CONISTON

24

Dodgson Wood

pier

pebble beach

Thrang Crag
Wood

Low Parkamoor

Cumbria Way

picnic area

25

Peel Islands

Blawith Fell

Selside Beck

BEACON
TARN

Bleak Knott

1 mile

25. Coniston Water and Beacon Tarn

An alternative route across Coniston Water adds in Beacon Tarn. From the picnic area and access point below Thrang Crag Wood swim straight across Coniston Water. Once across the field take the wooded path north and new forest road south on a zigzag route up to Selside Beck. Follow the track to Low Parkamoor and descend to Dodgson Wood.

Swim across Coniston Water to the pebble beach. Follow the Cumbria Way inland to Beacon Tarn. Beacon Tarn has large patches of surface weed to avoid, but is very pleasant for all that. In the summer the tarn is noticeably warmer than Coniston Water.

Swim east across the middle of the tarn. Follow the path north along Bleak Knott to Blawith Fell and northeast to the minor road that returns you to the picnic area.

There is much more to Coniston Water, including Peel Islands that lie just off the eastern bank about half way down the lake. (They are usually referred to as one island but in fact there are two, one large and one small, a few yards apart.) The twin islands have rocks for diving, and the larger one has well trodden paths. In *Swallows and Amazons* Peel Islands are the model for Wildcat Island and in the summer canoeists, dinghies and organised groups crowd in. On a warm day there is a faintly Mediterranean feel to the place.

Open Water Swimming

Open water swimming is rare in England, even amongst people who are physically active. How ever many sunbathers there are on a beach on a hot day, there will only be a few in the water, and these mostly children.

This reluctance to swim outside a chlorinated pool is odd, because the pleasure of open water swimming is not something that you grow out of, but grow into as you get older. A swimmer sometimes lives through each stage of this deepening enjoyment in the course of a single swim. The water is cold and you start by splashing around like a child. Then, like a teenager, you plunge into the water with bravado whoops as though you are doing something out of the ordinary and even a bit silly. As you swim a change takes place, which is inadequately described as 'getting used to the water'. It is not just that the physical shock of the cold water has worn off. Your mental state has changed; you mature. You become calm, you know that what you are doing is a natural and peaceable and good. If you have been walking or running, swimming becomes an easy, graceful extension of your journey. In a natural pool you become at one with your surroundings, in the sea you sense that you are connected to an infinite whole. When you feel like this, drowning holds no fear.

26. Seathwaite Tarn, Goat Water and Blind Tarn

This swimhike starts and finishes at Turner Hall Campsite. Unless you are also camping at the site there is no obvious carpark there or anywhere else on the route. But a good route need not be beholden to the car and a carpark certainly does not increase the route's aesthetic value, even if it makes it more convenient. A starting point only wants to feel like civilisation, and Turner Hall, a very pretty farmhouse, is certainly that. It is not, however, a hall but rather a cottage, and quite a small one.

From Turner Hall follow the duckboard path up the Duddon Valley, before turning northeast on the path and then over Black Allens to the northern side of Seathwaite Tarn. (Here the paths on the Ordnance Survey map are mostly imaginary). Aim to arrive opposite the nameless island just offshore. Swim to the island, climb over its steep slabs of rock and dive in again. The water here is deep and blue but resist the temptation to dive deep as swimsacs are only suitable for a shallow dive. Swim to the stones on the steep sided eastern shore. Just north of Studderstone How is a crag, long-faced, with a strip of green grass beneath. The grass is the natural and obvious line up, and it points almost exactly in the right direction--which is east.

Contour to Near Gill, rise in a curve to Far Gill and climb to Goat's Hawse. Goatwater appears below, hard up against the dramatic precipice of Dow Crag, so close that it is almost falling into the water. Descend to the stony lake and swim its length, then contour to the lip of Blind Tarn, nestled in a textbook corrie.

Blind Tarn is a perfect little place and is so small that it hardly matters where you get in and out. Take the track at the southern end which climbs past old mining huts and a deep cave. Continue up to Brown Pike and join the green lane called Walna Scar Road back down into the Duddon Valley. The final footpath back to Turner Hall Farm is full of chocolate brown rabbits.

Tarns around Coniston Old Man

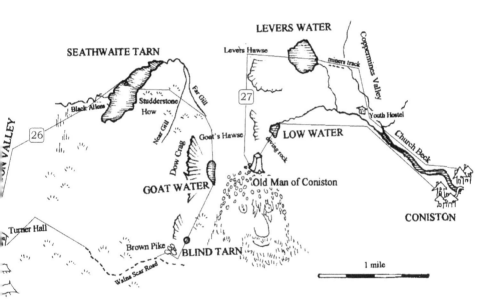

27. Levers Water and Low Water

From the shop on the corner in Coniston village follow the roads and paths on the north side of Church Beck. At the Youth Hostel, the path up the scree will take you direct to Levers Water, but better is to take the track up Coppermines Valley and then climb west up the curious raised miners track. This track rises dead straight past the entrances to the mines, not crude holes, but neat burrows rimmed by crafted stone. The breast of the hill is slightly higher than Levers Water.

Descend to Levers Water and enter at the large stone north of the weir. Swim west across the middle. Climb to the col at Levers Hawse and follow the ridge south to the Old Man of Coniston. Descend to Low Water and enter the lake from the diving rock at its southern bank. Swim north to the outlet and take the path back to the village. Be sure to keep on the south side of Church Beck so as not to cross your tracks. At the corner shop it is time to buy a well-earned snack.

Levers Water and Low Water are brother and sister. Twelve miles away they have two near-identical cousins, Blea Water and Small Water, who are almost exactly the same size, the same shape and the same distance from one another.

28. Blea Water and Small Water

This swimhike, not very taxing, provides a pleasant family day out. From the carpark at the end of Haweswater climb the path by Smallwater Beck to the lip of the lake. Skirt the southern bank and swim north across its centre. Climb the grass to the slight col on the lower slopes of Pilot Crag and contour down to the southern bank of Blea Water. Swim across and take one of the paths above Bleawater Beck back to the carpark.

What of the family? They can sit and picnic while you cross with the swimsac. This does, admittedly, make things slightly artificial. The point of a swimsac is to get in somewhere and to come out somewhere else. However, you will probably need to go back to the picnic site because--if your family is anything like mine--it will be *your* job to lug the picnic stuff around. But if you return to the picnic site, why not leave your stuff there? And in truth, on a hot day especially, it is rather pedantic to bother with a swimsac in these delightful tarns; you are better just frolicking in the water.

We took the route on a beautiful day in February. The valley was in thick mist and the car park was packed but, as is the mysterious way with packed carparks, the countryside was soon very peaceful. We climb through the fog hoping that it will clear, and, by great good fortune at the very lip of Small Water the mist roils and then ends abruptly; we are out into the blue. The family picnic, while I swim fully wetsuited, the cold water tastes delicious, and afterwards a cup of hot tea from the stove.

Looking down on Blea Water from above, it seems as if the northern half is covered in ice, but at the waters edge, the ice is invisible. Could I have imagined it? I swim to the middle. No, it is there. The edge of the ice is not jagged, but soft and blunted with dancing wavelets getting smaller and washing over the top and underneath and the water seeming to get thicker so that the boundary of ice and water is almost imperceptible. I do not touch the ice, it seems too beautiful, but swim beside it to the eastern outlet of the lake and to my family, who are having another picnic.

All this was in sunshine, but on the path back clouds reappeared over the brow, grew high and engulfed us in a matter of moments. My four year old son was nervous at the sudden cold clammy mist. It meant the Groke was coming! We must go! Now! I gave him the compass and told him to head south east, and he happily navigated us back down.

Rain and Wind

It is nice to swimhike in the sunshine, but do not be deterred by rain. Getting changed is, admittedly, inconvenient, but once you are in the water you realise that a relaxing and enveloping lake or tarn is much more enjoyable than walking along in the wet. Of course, you are wet in a lake too, but immersion in water it is a much nicer kind of wet than traipsing along with wet clothes feeling chilled by the air. With curtains of rain falling down it is a positive relief to enter the water and you will feel warmer in than out (though this is an illusion). Meanwhile your clothes are staying absolutely dry in the swimsac, at least until you have to get out again, and by then, with any luck, the rain will have stopped.

The impact of the wind depends on its direction. Swimming into a headwind with the waves breaking in your face the whole time is slow, unpleasant and tiring. Crosswinds are more manageable though waves may still buffet you. Best of all is when you are pushed briskly along by a wind blowing in the direction you want to go. Protected by the swimsac from the waves breaking behind, you are driven onto the far bank where the lake becomes a choppy sea splashing the shoreline with spray.

29. Haweswater

The inlet separating The Rigg from Old Corpse Road at the southern end of Haweswater seems rather piddling on the map when compared to the bulk of the lake. But looking down upon it from the road, you see that it is quite substantial, almost the size of Buttermere, and it is satisfying to reconnect the natural line between the spur jutting into the water at one side and the ancient burial pathway on the other.

From the road take the little path to the rocky shore on the south side of Rowantreethwaite Beck. Wood Howe Island, rocky with low trees, is a tempting diversion--were it not for the seagulls. Swim straight to The Rigg.

Climb through the trees to the path by the wall and ascend the ridge of Riggindale Crag to High Street. Thick mist closes in as I arrive at the summit. I stand still and listen to absolute silence. The sound of blood is in my ears, a sound I have barely heard since I was a child. This is the sound of silence for me. Eventually the silence is broken by a breeze, a lark and then by rain.

The rest of the route, Mardale Ill Bell, Nan Bield Pass, Harter Fell, Branstree and Selside Pike more or less follows the watershed. From Selside Pike join Old Corpse Road for the final descent. I aimed for Rowantreethwaite Well, but either did not find it, or found something too banal to be given a name.

131

The Big Idea Round 2
We wait for our moment of fame in the crypt of the Snees. Leonard Snee purchased the vault in 1740. In 1742 his daughter, aged 19, was the first member of the family to die and be buried within its chambers. The Big Idea crew have put sofas around the crypt and provided pastries and fruit, a distinct improvement on Round One where all we had was cups of tea.

There are six semi-finalists:
1. David and Maree have a cardboard potty
2. Geoff and Rachel have a 'Yes, I am single' bracelet.
3. Malcolm has gaiters.
4. I have the swimsac
5. David has a radiator leak detector
6. Julian has his bike pump.

We are allowed out of the crypt for a preview tour of the fabulous church being desecrated for the occasion: Christ Church near Liverpool Street Station in London, a Georgian masterpiece. We are told where to stand. The two minute pitch I have prepared for the occasion is not, in fact, required. This is a shame, as I had prepared a rather good story about a romantic couple going swimming and then coming out to find that their things have gone missing. It is explained that the three judges (Craig, Ruth and Karan) and the audience will see a film of Lieutenant Colonel Dick Strawbridge (another TV personality), 'test driving' each of the inventions before a question and answer session, in which our mentors will be rooting for us all the way.

We have supper on a double decker bus parked near the church and the show begins as one by one we are called up to be judged.

A TV has been installed in the crypt, but although we can hear the sound, only occasionally does the picture work. Malcolm is up first. His gaiters pass Lt. Col. Strawbridge's test rather well, but he is dealt with more harshly by the judges. David and Maree are next. The cardboard potty passes the 'test drive' and is subject to universal acclaim by the judges. Craig, has lots of bright ideas about using the potty as a dog's toilet and is behind them '100%'. This is bad news for me; Craig is 'mentoring' David and Maree as well as myself, and each mentor must ditch one of his two protégées as the six projects are whittled down to one at the climax of the show. Geoff and Rachel have a somewhat more rocky ride with their bracelet, and then it is me.

Applause. I shake hands and we all watch the test drive. Dick Strawbridge is dressed in a tuxedo. Now he is dressed in a wetsuit. He is swimming across a large pond. Oh No!--the swimsac is not strapped to his back as it is meant to be; it is held beneath his chest, army style, as he paddles across with his legs. 'I'm getting worried about this', he warns. 'There are lots of bubbles coming up'. On the far bank he empties the outer bag of pond water with an accusing look on his face. His tuxedo, he reports, is distinctly damp.

We have a conversation. Craig and Richard, the presenter, agree that what I need is a drybag with straps. Ruth asks Craig:

'But is it a Big Idea'?
'No'. Craig replies. 'I have to be honest. It's not'.

'How do you feel?' Richard asks me, 'being betrayed by your mentor'?

'He is just being honest. At least Dick Strawbridge didn't drown'. I quip.

'But it is you who are, metaphorically, drowning' says Richard, 'deserted by your mentor'.

I get into an aggressive argument with Richard. I squeak. I wave my arms mimicking crawl strokes. I insult the intelligence of Dick Strawbridge. I try to compress my two minute pitch into a few seconds as Richard looks on, unsmiling. The romantic couple, swimming, the missing clothes…

'I'll tell you what's not romantic', says Richard, 'swimming around with a rucksack on your back'!

This raises a laugh.

'It makes no difference!' I squeak. 'It's physics'!

Oh dear.

When I come back down to the crypt, everyone is silent.

'At least now I can relax', I say.

Julian and his cycle pump go through to the next round.

Devoke Water

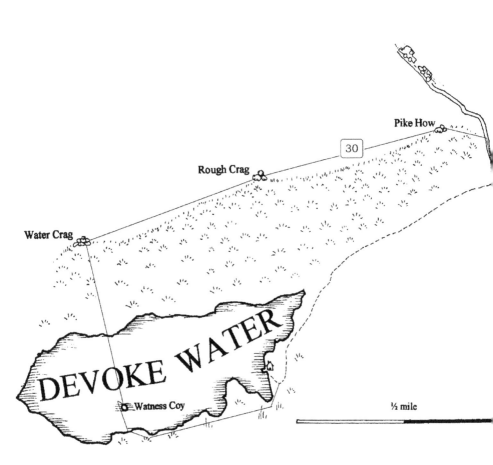

30. Devoke Water

Situated on its own, Devoke Water might naturally be crossed on a long linear route along the western flanks of the Lake District, but can also be visited in a short circular swimhike. From just below Pike How take the road south to join the bridleway west to Devoke Water. At the lake an old water board house has been built jutting into the water and the track peters out. Skirt the southern shore until you are opposite Watness Coy, a bushy, brackeny, little island thick with vegetation and with two or three stunted windblown trees. Swim the shallow gap to skirt the island, pretty waterplants flourish on its edges. Do not attempt to land further than the natural stone seat beneath the mountain ash on the island's north side.

Swim to Devoke Water's north shore, climb the easy open ground to Water Crag and follow the path west along the ridge, peeling off to take in the summit of Rough Crag before returning to Pike How and the road.

A Good Route

Plato suggested that everything has its ideal form. There is an ideal form of chair, there is an ideal form of government, there is an ideal form of swimsac and there is an ideal form of route. By imagining what an ideal route is like we can aim, more modestly, to create a good route. A good route starts and ends at a village or some other point of habitation. (To start on a road is a little unsatisfactory, as you are already *on* a route.) The route then has three qualities:

(1) It follows a natural line. Sometimes a natural line is the line of least resistance, the genius of a sheep track contouring across a mountainside. But a natural line need not always be the easiest way; it can also be a geographical feature with a self-defined path like a ridge or a river.

(2) Each step—or stroke—is its own pleasure. The pleasure may be the view, or just the physical sensation of being immersed in a lake, or of heather brushing against your legs.

(3) It reaches high points—literally and figuratively. All routes require high points so that there is something to aim at, to maintain the illusion that the journey is necessary (which if course it is not). A high point is a mountain peak, but it can be anything of beauty, or interest. It might be a sudden view or a curiously shaped rock. It can be natural, like a waterfall, or manmade like a church.

How do these principles apply to swimming on a swimhike?

If a swim is quicker than going round the edge of a lake or bay, then it is a natural line. By the same token a route that takes advantage of promontories to reduce the distance of the swim is natural. Swimming across the middle of a long lake, therefore, is natural: it is efficient and time saving. Following the line of a lake from one end to the other, like following a river, is also natural line. But it may not be the most enjoyable route to take. Swimming is pleasurable, but the pleasure can pall as the distance increases. So the longer the distance of the swim, the more important it is that it is quicker and easier to reach the next highpoint by water rather than on foot.

Crossing water has its own highpoints. They include islands; they can include a particularly nice beach or diving rock going in or out of the water, and they can include the view from the water, which is often particularly fine from the centre of a lake. Less predictably encounters with wildlife (ospreys, seals) can also be high points.[*]

Out and back, linear, and circular routes
The line that is followed determines whether a good route requires at least one, two or three highpoints (although there is no harm in having more).

An out and back route requires *one* high point. This, of course, is the last point that you reach before you retrace the way you have come. If you are climbing a mountain it is the top.

A point to point route requires *two* high points: where you start and where you finish. Sea to sea routes exemplify this.

A circular route requires *three* high points to justify the circle. The start and finish of a circular route does not need to be a highpoint: you can join the circle anywhere.

The circular swimhikes in this book have been planned with the principles of a good route in mind, although, sometimes I have compromised them somewhat.

---

[*] or low points (seagulls).

Eskdale

31. Blea Tarn, Burnmoor Tarn and Stony Tarn

In the Esk Valley there is a small carpark at the Beckfoot Access Area below Dalegarth Station. Follow the path downstream and then a short stretch of road to Boot Station. Climb the path to the south end of Blea Tarn. Swim the length of the tarn to the north end, where it has its own little mountain, Blea Hill. Climb the false summit of Blea Hill and cut down to join the path north east for half a mile or so. There are rocks along the way. Look out for a final rocky outcrop, about eight feet high, overlooking Brat's Moss, a shallow marshy valley. From the outcrop look again! There below you are three stone circles, all quite close to each other and very distinct. The stones are set in marsh but have inner patterns that create grassy ridges and—somewhat unusually for stone circles—each has its own central stone in addition to the ring around the edge.

What is going on? Each circle represents a lake, and the stones in the middle are the centres of the lakes. But which three lakes might they be? Our three lakes! The natural connection between Blea Tarn, Burnmoor Tarn and Stony Tarn is beautifully expressed in the three circles that lie almost exactly equidistant between them.[*]

Join the track northeast up the southern flank of Miterdale. Beneath you the natural course comes to a sudden and unexpected halt in cliffs and the river that feeds the valley appears at right angles, pouring down from Illgill Head.

---

[*] I could not find two more circles indicated on the map towards Low Longrigg. The circles cannot be very prominent and probably represent Siney Tarn and Eel Tarn, shallow, reedy and no good for swimming.

Continue northeast to Burnmoor Tarn. Follow the marshy northwest shore until half way along the tarn before swimming east across the middle. (If entering the tarn from here feels a bit nebulous and arbitrary; you may wish to get in as soon as you arrive at the southern end and swim past the Lodge to the shallow bay on the northeast bank.)

Descend Whillan Beck to Lambford Bridge, skirt Eskdale Fell and take a rising contour to Stony Tarn nestled in bumpy hills. Swim south over Stony Tarn; it is shallow with underwater reeds rising from between the stones. Climb Whin Crag and pick up a path of sorts beneath Peelplace Noddle. This takes you south to the road at the Woolpack Inn. Join the path down the River Esk. At the near end, Doctor Bridge is fun for paddling. And at the far end you reach Saint Catherine's Church, a quintessential Lake District Church, very beautiful and peaceful with the noise of the river murmuring faintly outside. From the Church the path returns you to the road just above Beckfoot.

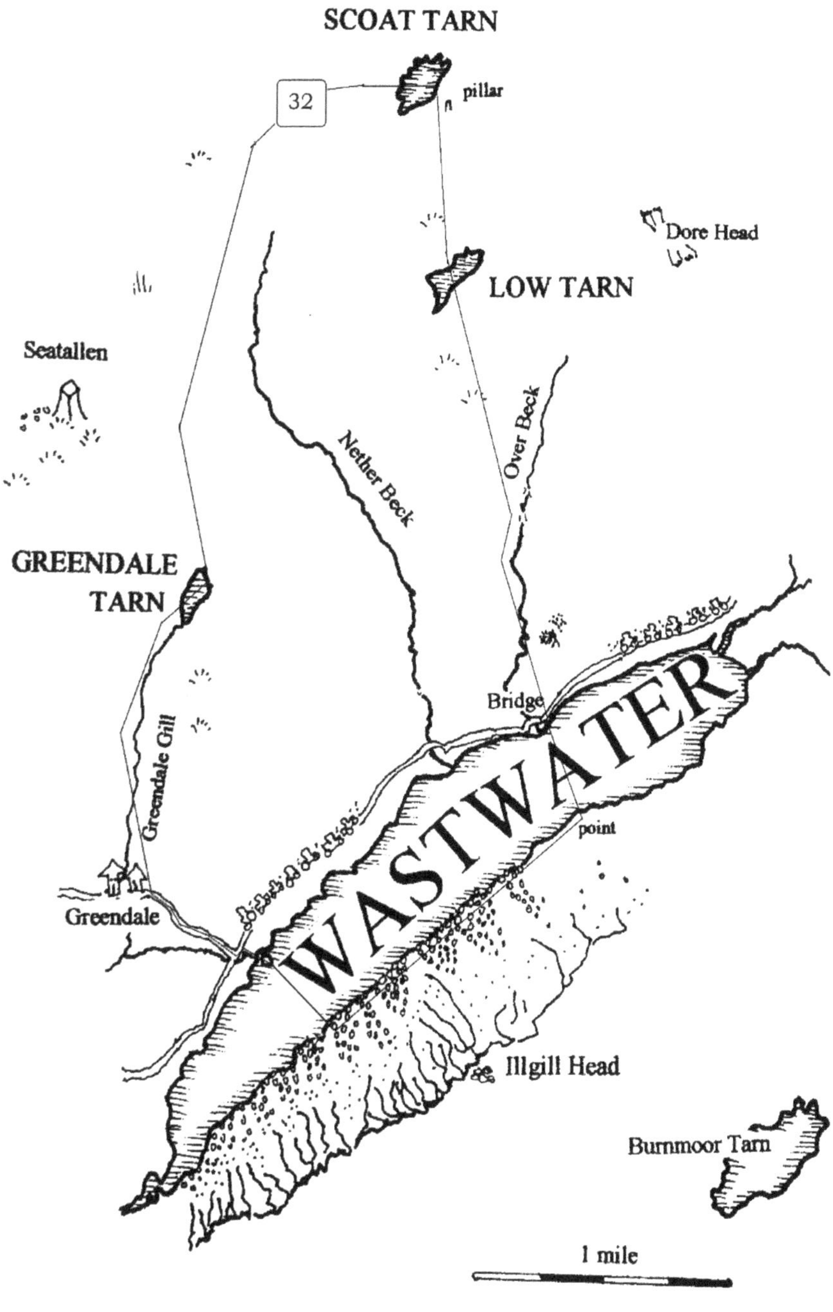

SCOAT TARN

pillar

32

Dore Head

Seatallen

LOW TARN

Nether Beck

Over Beck

GREENDALE TARN

Greendale Gill

Bridge

WASTWATER

point

Greendale

Illgill Head

Burnmoor Tarn

1 mile

32. Wastwater, Low Tarn, Scoat Tarn and Greendale Tarn

Wastwater has a little island at the road junction below Greendale. It is misrepresented as a peninsula by the Ordnance Survey, but an island it is, only to be reached by stepping stones. Step out onto the island and swim straight for the eastern bank beneath Illgill Head. Soon the shallows are left behind and the water beneath becomes very blue and very deep. Up the valley is the celebrated view so beloved of advertisers.

Land on the eastern shore where the Wasdale Screes 'make their unhalting plunge'.* Luckily for swimhikers there is, in fact, a three foot ledge along the shoreline before the jumble of rocks, now covered in a thin layer of soft brown algae, continue steeply down until they disappear into the blue-black of the lake.

Take the path across the screes north for a mile to the unnamed Point where Scafell comes into view. On the opposite shore is humpbacked Overbeck Bridge. Swim to the stony beach north of the bridge.

At this point the reader interjects:

'Hey! I have swam across Wastwater, hiked a mile over scree and then swam back. What's the point of that? Surely I should have visited a mountain or something'?

How long have I stared at the map trying to overcome this problem! But try as I might I can think of no better alternative for a circular route. Armed with a wetsuit you can swim north

---

* Auden and Isherwood, *The Ascent of F6*

up the length of Wastwater as an alternative to swimming across it.* However, even with the amazing view, the experience starts to pall after a mile or so, and you find yourself looking wistfully at the bank. Possibly after crossing Wastwater you could head over to Burnmoor Tarn, but then how do you return? Another option—which I have not tried—might be to climb Wasdale Screes to Illgill Head. But even if this climb is possible it looks extremely unpleasant—even nastier than climbing a footway. So I leave the discovery of a better route to you, the reader, and to future generations of swimhikers.

The double crossing of Wastwater is now complete, but there are still three tarns to visit. Really you are just heading for one of them, the lovely Scoat Tarn, but to fully appreciate her preeminent virtues, call in on her ugly sisters, Low Tarn and Greendale Tarn. Be careful; these two tarns are jealous of the beautiful tarn above them and both will try and detain you with reeds that rise up out of their shallow water to wrap around your hands and face.

From the bridge climb the path above the glistening pools and sunny grass banks of Over Beck. At the penultimate waterfall cut north over open grassy terrain up to Low Tarn. As you climb, the mountains each side of Dore Head create a natural frame for the summit of Great Gable. Swim north across the middle of Low Tarn. Patches of reed are unavoidable; overarm strokes are best to loosen the clinging fronds from your arms.

---

* As has been mentioned, I once tried to swim the length of Wastwater without a wetsuit in early June, with disastrous results.

Climb north to the ridge and there below you is Scoat Tarn, deep and blue. Sellafield nuclear power station, which has also just come into view, glowers in the distance, but its ugliness and the appalling threat it poses serves only to increase the rare beauty of the tarn.* A little above Scoat Tarn is a small, precarious looking pillar of rock about eight feet high. I hardly dared touch it, it looked about to collapse at any second, but it was solid.**

Half way down the eastern bank of Scoat Tarn there is a miniature cliff that rises to about four foot above the water. It is ideal for a shallow dive. The water is cold.

Exit Scoat Tarn from the shallows of the western back and contour above Nether Beck and below Seatallen to Greendale Tarn. Swim diagonally down from the eastern shoulder to about the western knee of the tarn avoiding the reeds as best you can. Descend Greendale Gill to join the road just east of the cottages at Greendale. The road takes you back to the junction and to the island in the lake.

---

* By the time this is published most of the above-ground concrete structures at Sellafield will hopefully have been flattened, and the view will revert to green fields (*Note to 2nd Edn*: dream on), albeit ones concealing several thousand tons of glowing radioactive sludge.
** This is generally true of rocks in the Lake District. However remote a place appears, thousands have been there before you and prodded and trodden on and climbed up all the rocks until the loose ones have all been firmly put into place. You get so used to it that it is a shock in a truly wild place, like the Highlands of Scotland, to tread on a large rock and find it shifting under your foot. The first thought as you wobble is not fear but a rush of indignation: 'Oy! What's going on?'

The Search for Arcadia

Which of all the tarns is the best, most beautiful, most lovely place to swim? The question is misguided. It is more than likely that by the time you have climbed to a tarn you have already gone past the ideal spot. From the lips of the tarns, fast flowing rivers tumble down through perfect pools, a string of pearls. Clear and sparkling water rushes laughing from one pool to the next. There is no need for a swimsac; on a warm summer's day, every pool is its own small heaven, and you only have to step down off the path to find it.

Surprisingly few adults take advantage of these little patches of paradise sprinkled below them. Some may sit and picnic while their children and dogs enjoy the water. Most continue to labour upwards on the path or painful footway. Where are they going? What impels them on past innumerable delights, what endless journey are they on?

There are many more routes for the swimhiker to explore in the Lake District, but we cannot potter around there forever. It is time to cross the Pennines to North East England. The area has its own mountains and even a few lakes, although there is nothing to compare with the high Lake District rivers. The characteristic North East river is big, brown, dirty and slow moving. Not paradise exactly, but these rivers do hold one advantage to us: we can swim down them.

North East England

SCOTLAND

NORTH

Holy Island 12

10

11

EAST

2   5 6

3

Druridge Bay

Hadrian's Wall   4   Newcastle

Sunderland 1

9

Durham 7 8

ENGLAND

THE

LAKE DISTRICT

30 miles

NORTH EAST ENGLAND

The most remarkable natural feature of North East England is its fine coastline of cliffs and long sandy beaches. The early morning can be especially beautiful as the sun rises over the sea and illuminates the spray of the waves. North East England also has some marvellous upland scenery from where its great rivers draw their waters. Below the moors and mountains lies pleasant farmland and a considerable number of towns and villages. The urban areas are sometimes rather cruelly described as being aesthetically challenged and certainly they lack the dainty old-world-charm sometimes found of southern England. However, the North East is not lacking a past and has an abundance of superb historic sites. It is this great legacy that is explored in these swimhikes. We will visit places that range from Durham Cathedral and Hadrian's Wall, to less well known spots: a Neolithic stone circle, a lime kiln, a Victorian park.

When reaching a cathedral, castle or some other great monument afoot, one feels a deep sense of connection with the past. The feeling of awe and awareness of the spirit of the place is far more intense than if you have merely shuffled in from the nearest carpark. (How much better it would be if everyone had to walk 10 miles to reach Stonehenge!) Follow these routes and you will discover that to visit a historic site after having hiked *and swam* there, gives an experience that is deeper and richer still.

When compared to the Lake District, upland lakes in North East England are few and far between, and are often designated as reservoirs where swimming is 'forbidden' (although Derwent Reservoir hosts a triathlon).[*] This, of course, in no way invalidates our natural right to swim in these lakes, but as it happens our quest to explore north east history means that most of the swimhikes described here follow rivers and the sea. This is less safe than lake swimming. The rivers are interspersed with rapids, the water is murky and there are underwater snags. The sea is polluted with sewage and jetskis. There are also waves, tides, currents and offshore winds and it is a long way to Denmark. In truth the sea can be dangerous, certainly more dangerous than the alleged risks of a reservoir, although because nobody owns the sea nobody cares overmuch if you swim in it. But I do not want to put you off; the North East offers tremendous routes for the swimhiker.

South Bents to Roker

The route from South Bents around the North Pier to the inner beach at Roker is not a numbered swimhike, as I completed it before inventing the swimsac.

On a beautiful April morning I set out for a swim (in my wetsuit) leaving my clothes, shoes, towel and house keys in a rucksack on the shore at South Bents. I jogged back up the beach a couple of hours later to find that my rucksack was missing.

A middle-aged couple watched me for a minute or two as I searched amongst the seagrass, then the man said:

'Are you looking for a blue rucksack?'
'Yes!'
'Well it's not there anymore. There's been a suicide and the police have taken it away.'
'I have *not* committed suicide', I said, but the couple were both adamant that I had, or at least that someone had.

Police hunt for rucksack owner

Police are anxious to hear from the person who left a rucksack on the beach at Seaburn.

The bag, containing swimwear and socks, was found on the sand opposite the Bay Hotel.

The owner can pick the rucksack up at Southwick police station.

This police announcement in the *Sunderland Echo* is rather misleading. The article states, correctly, that the rucksack contained socks. However, it fails to mention that it contained all my other clothes as well. And the rucksack did not, in fact, contain any swimwear, because I was wearing it.

152

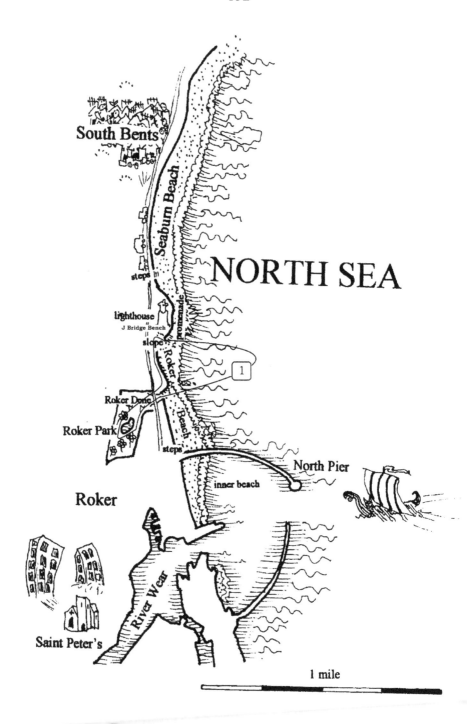

1. Roker

A useful mimetic for the north east coast is that *the tide flows to Flamborough, and ebbs to Edinburgh.* As it is safer to swim on an incoming tide than an outgoing one, it is better, on the whole, to swim south for Flamborough. But when swimhiking from Roker in Sunderland there is a certain logic to going north. On the short route, a quick swim takes you around a cliff. Once you are around you can choose how far to swim before exiting on the sand. On the longer route that takes you past the promenade, you have had a considerable opportunity to gage swimming conditions along a sandy beach where you can get out at any time before deciding whether or not to continue along a final rocky section of the shore.

The short route is best done at high tide, to gain the satisfaction of swimming around the base of the cliff. From the seafront below Roker Dene Bridge swim straight out to sea (there are one or two rocks to avoid below the cliff) and then swim north round the cliff to exit where the promenade slopes up out of the beach. Climb the steps and follow the cliff path to the zebra crossing at the entrance to Roker Park. On the way you can see cannonball limestone, the circular bases of two great guns, a cross to Bede, a naval mine, and John Bridge's bench. Explore the park's fine Victorian landscaping, the model boat lake, scented garden, bandstand and little wooden bridge. Follow the path down Roker Dene under the road bridge and back to the seafront.

I recommend this short route. The combination of a swim beneath the cliff, the cliff path, the park and dene strikes a pleasant balance. The longer route, which starts at the beach by the North Pier, is less distinctive, but does serve to illustrate how, with the help of a swimsac, you can swim in one direction and walk or jog back along more or less any beach. Do not attempt this longer route in wavy water at high tide; the exit steps will be battered by the sea.

Descend the steps north of the pier, take a diagonal route to the sea to avoid rocks and swim north for the first set of steps at Seaburn Beach. Be sure of yourself before continuing past the start of the promenade; depending on the state of the sand there may be a rocky shore that it would not do to climb out on in waves. At Seaburn a confluence of currents may slow you down. Watch for patches of kelp, their brown cadaverous arms rearing up as the waves recede. Some patches are unavoidable to swim over; keep your limbs high. After you have come out the water, climb the Seaburn steps and return past the lighthouse along the cliff path.

Half a mile from Roker Beach, Saint Peter's Church stands, rather forlornly, in a large square graveyard behind the university. It can be reached from the sea by taking the C2C cyclepath that follows the Wear estuary. St. Peter's was founded in 674, and was frequented by the Venerable Bede when he was a teenager. It survived the depredations of the Vikings, who tried to burn it down before they decided to settle—their descendants still live in the overarching tower blocks to the north. If the church is open you are sure to receive a most friendly welcome and perhaps be offered a tour of the sights: the doorway used by Bede and Cuthbert, the scorch marks from the Vikings, the two headed dragon, the homemade raspberry jam. But the church is all too often shut.* A sad proclamation nailed to the locked wooden door explains that stolen lead is to be replaced; an anti-climb barrier

---

* *Note to 2nd Edn* Happily the Church is now open regularly and offers lunch.

to be fitted to the Chapter House roof, and a security light and sensor installed on the east wall of the north transept.

The Need for a Swimsac

The idea of a swimsac was born when the police took my clothes away after my 'suicide'. But it was not the only occasion when something went wrong on a swim. One evening my clothes were hidden by jeering youths; on more than one morning a dog weed on them. In London lifeguards refused to allow me to leave a small bag of valuables by the side of Hampstead Pond: I had to leave them in the unguarded changing rooms so they could be stolen—that was *the rule*. In Dorset I swam point-to-point from Osmington Mills to Weymouth, where my Grandmother had kindly offered to meet me beneath the clock tower with a bag of clothes. I came out of the sea at the clock tower at the very time I had anticipated, feeling pleased with my precision, and rather thirsty. My Grandmother was not there.[*] I encountered one problem after another until in the end I was more or less forced to invent the swimsac. The swimsac came into being, not because I wanted one, but because I *needed* one.

Hillary Clinton

Perhaps the most famous person to have found herself in need of a swimsac is Hillary Clinton. On her last day at college, Hillary Rodham, as she then was, took a fond farewell of its lake, unaware that malignant eyes were watching her.

Later that afternoon, I took one last swim in Lake Waban ... I stripped down to my bathing suit and left my cut-off

---

[*] Eventually I found her in a teashop at Melcombe Regis.

jeans and T-shirt in a pile on the shore with my aviator like glasses on top. I didn't have a care in the world as I swam out towards the middle, and because of my nearsightedness, my surroundings looked like an Impressionist painting. I have loved being at Wellesley and had taken great solace in all seasons from its natural beauty. The swim was a final goodbye. When I got back to shore I couldn't find my clothes or my glasses.

I finally had to ask a campus security officer if he had seen any belongings. He told me that President Adams had seen me swimming ... and had directed him to confiscate them.[*]

Thus was the enmity between Hillary Clinton and the forces of conservatism sealed. If only she had had a swimsac with her then the whole course of political history might have been different.

Rescue

In the summer at Sunderland there are lifeguards and they quite often come out in a boat to rescue me, although I do not, in fact, need rescuing. Looking back at these rescue missions I feel a sense of gratitude. In a world that is all too often cruel, it is nice to be reminded of people who will set out to save their fellow human beings, and somehow touching that this includes me. At the time of the rescues, however, my only feelings are of irritation, although I do my best to sound polite when explaining that help is not needed. In other seasons, I can generally swim in peace, although I am never wholly safe.

---

[*] Hillary Clinton, *Living History*, Headline 2003, p. 42.

It is a wet day in early December. The Wear is in flood, and great waves are breaking over Roker's North Pier. But within the sheltered inner beach the waves are gentle, well within the margin of safety. The beach is empty. 'Good'! I think, 'No dogs to wee on my clothes! Now get changed quick'! Shoes off. Socks off and into shoes. Glasses off and into a shoe. Shirt off and stuffed in both shoes. Done! I run down the beach in my tri-shorts; I have the vague intimation of being watched.

I wade into the brown water and swim through the matted sticks brought down by the flood and out into the bay, where I alternate swimming on my front and back. Even further out, the water is brown and a bit repellent, and I soon retreat to the shore. It is not the cold; the water is just too smelly to stay in longer.

I dress quickly and decide on a whim to run the long way back, past the small pier. As I reach the marina a trim man steps out, calls to me and shows me his card. He is a police officer, off-duty. I have been swimming and he has called the emergency services. A search is underway. I apologise. 'I am alright. I just enjoy it', I explain. He thought at first that I was just going to swim straight back out again, and then, when I didn't, he said to her [there must have been two of them watching] that I *probably* would, but that I didn't look like a very good swimmer and that I looked like I was in difficulties. Then, after I *had* got out, he said, it was like I had noticed them and went running off the other way on purpose.

I apologise again and say that it was good of him to be vigilant.

'Well, the police deal with all sorts, including people who do stupid things'.

'I am *not* stupid…' I begin, but the officer is not listening, he is talking into his radio, explaining that he is with me and that I am alright: 'an athlete, an extreme athlete…'.

Another policeman turns up and I am escorted to a patrol car. Would I like to sit in it? No thank you, I would not like to get the seat wet. I have a chat, my apologies at having inconvenienced the police are relayed to the inspector, and I jog on. I rather liked being called an extreme athlete and I liked how, on the principle of better-safe-than-sorry, the officers did not hesitate to interfere in a friendly way. It would be annoying, though, if it happened too often.

On one occasion I came embarrassingly close to really being rescued. The waves were large and coming at all angles and I swam out to lark around in them, foolishly oblivious to the current that was pulling me south towards an area where my way back to Roker Beach was cut off by rocks. A summer lifeguard speared out through the surf on a paddle board to rescue me and I swam in to reassure him. Only then did I realise how far I had been pulled. I was tired when I reached him and tempted to grab his board. But I didn't.

Afterwards I tried to analyse why I had not noticed what was happening, even though the pull had been obvious almost from the moment I stepped into the water. All I could come up with was that being tossed around amongst the waves was so intensely enjoyable that I forgot all about it. Perhaps I *am* a bit stupid.

Harbottle

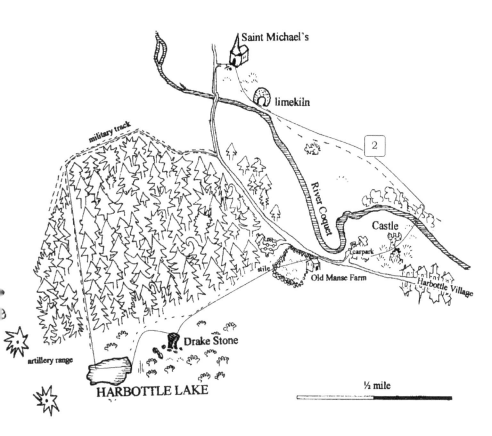

2. Harbottle Lake

This swimhike links five highpoints within a loop of about three miles. The first is the old ruined castle on a hillock overlooking Harbottle village street. It has its own carpark, is always open and is free to visit. From the castle ruins descend north to the River Coquet. From the southern river bank, delightful for picnicking, wade to the wood on the north shore. Natural stepping stones span the river, but in between the water is three foot deep. Climb through the wood to the bridleway. Head west, watch for red squirrels. A superbly crafted limekiln set into the hill and looking like a gigantic round beehive provides the second highpoint.

From the bridleway cut over the field to the southwest corner of Saint Michael's Church, large and beautiful, the third high point. Inside homemade marmalade is on sale. Surely this contravenes EU regulations? Old gravestones are used to flag the path down to the road, one with the skull and cross bones etched deeply into the stone. Pirates must have borrowed the Jolly Roger from graves such as these, or was it the other way around?

Take the road south and join the military track westward. Near the track I found a crow in a cage. I went to free it. Next to the cage there was a notice:

> The Ministry of Defence, in its conservation program, needs to protect ground nesting birds from carrion crows and other predators. These humane and legal traps are checked at least once a day. Do not tamper with them.

So I left the crow to its fate.

Take the footpath south along the line of the fence through the wood. This brings you out on the north shore of Harbottle Lake, the centre of the lake being the fourth highpoint. The junction of the path and lake provides a good entry point on firm sand and stone. Beyond this point are forbidding notices warning of the artillery range. Swim east down the lake to exit on the eastern bank. Ahead of you is the cap of the fifth and final highpoint, the Drake Stone, a huge boulder. It is tempting to beeline direct over rough heather for the Stone, but easier to loop north to take advantage of the path and ridge.

At the southern end of the Drake Stone's eastern face there are steps cut into the rock. They are not too difficult to climb up, but just because you can climb up something, *it does not mean that you can climb back down again.*[*] It would be an ignominious fate to get stuck on top of a boulder; you will probably be rescued eventually, but who knows?

Return (if you are not stuck) to the path east down the hill. An unmarked stone stile allows a short cut across the field to Old Manse Farm, one hundred yards up the road from the entrance to the grounds of the castle.

A couple of miles South of Harbottle there appears to be an embarrassment of historical riches at Holywell, including Lady's Well, St. Mungo's Well and Rob Roy's cave. The cave, however, is fenced off and according to the lady at the nearby farm there is not much to see anyway. St Mungo's Well is merely a running faucet set in a block of stone by the

---

[*] If you are anything like me, it is probably no use just being told this. You will have to learn it, again and again, through bitter practical experience.

road. Still, the round pool of Lady's Well is certainly worth seeing. I was hoping also to swim in it, but discovered that it serves the village for drinking water and is, besides, only six inches deep.

Darden

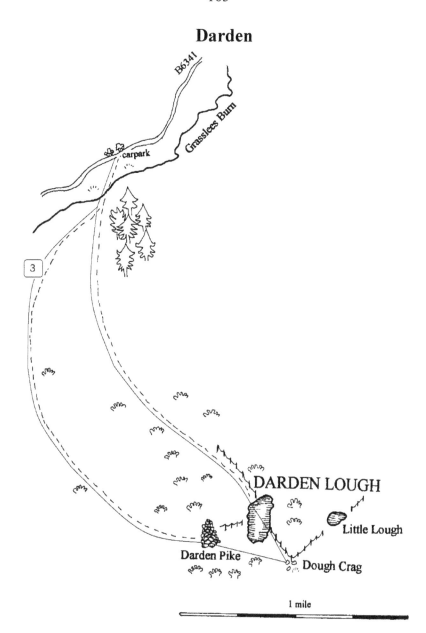

B6341

Grasslees Burn

carpark

3

DARDEN LOUGH

Little Lough

Darden Pike

Dough Crag

1 mile

164

3. Darden Lough

Visiting this wonderful and remote lough provides a very satisfying swimhike. Not only is the lough of great beauty, but getting there involves a good climb, and the nearby summits provide spectacular views over Northumberland. However, there are no historical monuments nearby, unless you count an ancient cairn on one of the hills above the lough. What then shall we do with our rule that every north east swimhike must include a historical monument? On this one occasion, we shall simply ignore it.

Two miles to the north of Darden Lough there is a small carpark on the B6341. From here, a quick dogleg south over Grasslees Burn brings you to the start of a circular marked route to the lough. The Darden Lough swimhike simply follows that loop, with a modest diversion to swim the across the lough and to climb Dough Crag.

Taking the route clockwise, climb the path south to the lough. Watch for adders. Enter the water on the western shore 70 yards south of the fence, where the heather turns to grass. There is a firm peaty entry. Swim southeast through peat red water to exit on the steep bank by the fence. Climb the high point of Dough Crag before cutting west over heather and rough ground to Darden Pike with its old cairn. Descend the path north to complete the loop.

When the reader consults the map, they can hardly fail to notice that not half a mile east of Darden Lough is another lough, called Little Lough. If Darden Lough is a delight, then what joy might Little Lough also contain? Surely the swimhike should be extended to cross this lough too?

Here is a case in which a guidebook can really prove its worth.

DO NOT SWIM ACROSS LITTLE LOUGH.

If you do, you will come out coated in mud.

Hadrian's Wall

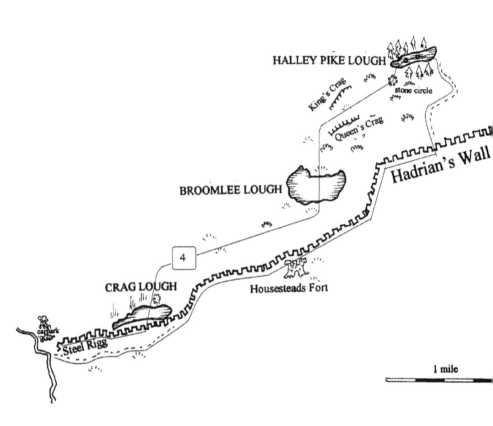

4. Hadrian's Loughs

Hadrian's Wall, dividing north and south, also connects the North East to the Lakes, in a natural line of wave-like hills over the Pennines. Here the eye is captured by the line of the Wall and the beautiful scattering of loughs lie unnoticed. There are seven in the space of a few miles and this swimhike takes in three of them.

From Steel Rigg follow Hadrian's Wall east. Where the trees begin below, make the steep descent to Crag Lough. Swim across the middle to the fence and tree promontory on the far bank. There may be nesting swans amongst the rushes to the west; give them room. The centre of the lough is reedy and the far bank is waterlogged.

Make your way by the eastbound path and open ground to the south shore of Broomlee Lough. Watch for deer. Swim to the flat stone shelf at the shallow north shore. Climb over walls and down the valley between King and Queen's crags to the stone circle, a small circumference but with some quite large stones poking above the heather.

Descend to the south shore of Halley Pike Lough. Swim to the two man-made islands of stone, presumably from the Wall. (The islands are not marked on the Ordnance Survey 1.50,000 map.) Both islands are thick with trees and the western island has rhododendron. Swim back to the shore and join the path south to Hadrian's Wall.

Follow the line of Wall back to Steel Rigg. At the eastern end of Crag Lough take the lower path to avoid retracing your steps.

Part way along the Wall is Housesteads Fort. Admission is by ticket and in this car-centred world the only place to buy a ticket is next to the car park some way below. There is no honesty box at the Wall, so swimhikers of impeccable moral rectitude will have to take an irritating dogleg down the shuffle path and through the gift emporium to the ticket office. For more lawless spirits, the Fort can easily be breached from the Wall, except on popular summer days when it is vigorously defended by the uniformed foot soldiers of English Heritage.

The Assyrians

> The Assyrian came down like the wolf on the fold,
> And his cohorts were gleaming in purple and gold.[*]

It cannot have been very pleasant to have been on the receiving end of the Assyrians. In the ninth century BC their leader King Ashurnasirpal fought an extensive campaign depicted on stone panels that are now in the British Museum. Towns are captured; there are long lines of prisoners; crows pick at corpses—or are they seagulls? In the first recorded instance of a ball game, soldiers play catch with enemy heads.

Amidst all the carnage a curious detail emerges. Look carefully at one of the lower panels and you see that one of

---

[*]Byron, *The Destruction of Sennacherib*.

the soldiers is loading things into a goatskin.[*] Then several Assyrians can be seen swimming naked across the Euphrates with the inflated goatskins gripped beneath them. Where are their clothes and weapons? Inside the goatskins of course! The Assyrians had invented a kind of swimsac and the panels record a swimhike.

Assyrian Swimhikers

Swimhikers can use all four main strokes

John Bridge

With its beautiful domed church, the island of St Georgio's, just across the water from St Mark's Square, is one of the finishing touches that gives Venice its magic. During the Second World War, however, the island concealed a sinister secret: it was the training ground and headquarters of the Meereskämpfer or MK 700, a clandestine espionage group of Nazi swimhikers, In September 1944 the twelve men of Einsatz Gruppe 1 of the MK700 were transported by rail across war-torn Europe to the River Waal (the main branch of The Rhine Delta) a few miles upriver from Nijmegan in Holland. Nijmegan had just been liberated with its bridges over the Waal intact. The fleeing Nazis had tried to blow the bridges up, but had failed because a young resistance fighter, Jan van Hoof, had cut the detonation wires. Thwarted by the heroic van Hoof, the Nazis were now sending their swimhikers to destroy them.

The group swam downriver into the night, pushing three bombs. They reached the road and rail bridges undetetected and attached the explosives to them. Ten of them were then captured by Sergeant George Rowson and his squad. (One of the swimhikers was wearing an expensive watch. Sgt Rowson took it for a souvenir and his son later sold it for a tidy sum.)

Two of the Nazi bombs blew up and damaged but did not destroy the bridges. A third was still down in the water, where it threatened to detonate at any moment. There was only one thing to do: fly in Lieutenant Commander John Bridge.

Lt Cdr Bridge was a man of extraordinary daring. A bomb disposal expert, he had already cleared the mines from Messina Harbour in Sicily, for which he had won the George Cross. He had also won the George Medal, twice.

Lt Cdr Bridge swam down into the murky water and felt his way towards the bomb, which was attached to a cable. He managed to loop a wire around it, and then had it manoeuvred out of the water and into a boat, where he defused it. The bridges were saved! Lt Cdr Bridge was not given another medal for this. It was thought that he had enough already.

After the War was over, Lt Cdr Bridge GC GM Bar became Director of Education in Sunderland and could often be found enjoying a walk along its seafront. He is commemorated by a bench at Roker, which can be visited on the Roker swimhike (No. 1, Short Route) on the cliff path between the steps and the zebra crossing.

Hetton Lyons Country Park

It is a sunny Saturday morning in September. Me and my son, aged 8, and Kevin and his two boys take the inflatable canoe down to the beach and start to blow it up. JP, who has been sat watching us from a beached canoe, comes over.

JP: Excuse Me. You can't canoe here.
Peter: Can't canoe in Hetton Lyons Lake?
JP: This lake is private.
Kevin: Private? Who owns it?
JP: Sunderland City Council.
Kevin: So it's public then.
JP: We [Springboard Adventure] manage it for Sunderland City Council, and you can't canoe here; you don't have life jackets.
Peter: We do have *a* life jacket.
JP: You don't have a life jacket and you haven't booked.

Peter: [looks out over empty lake]. Alright. We don't mind booking. We'll go and book.

JP: You can't book because you haven't got insurance.

Peter and Kevin: Insurance!

JP: Yes. You need insurance.

Peter: Well, what do we need insurance for? We're not going to start suing our own family members.

JP: Exactly, we're liable and you haven't got insurance. [Pause] There. Now I've told you. That means we're liable. So now you definitely can't go in. If I were you I'd go somewhere nearby.

Peter: Where?

JP: Roker Beach on an inshore breeze. No one will bother you there.

Peter: [incredulous] The North Sea! That's far more dangerous!

JP [as though I were trying to catch him out on a legal technicality]: I'm not saying which is more dangerous. I'm not saying if it's Roker Beach or this lake.

Peter: I've been in the lake lots of times and never had a problem.

JP: Five years we've been in charge. Do you *know* about this lake?

Peter [correctly guessing his drift]: Yes. It's getting weedy. But the weeds aren't a problem.

JP: It's weedy. Twelve-foot weeds.

We give up. JP returns to his beached canoe. A man walks down to the water and his dog bounds in. We make loud ironic comments. 'Has that dog booked'? 'Is it insured'? 'Look! It's not wearing a life jacket'! But they do nothing to relieve the bitterness of defeat.

Warkworth Hermitage

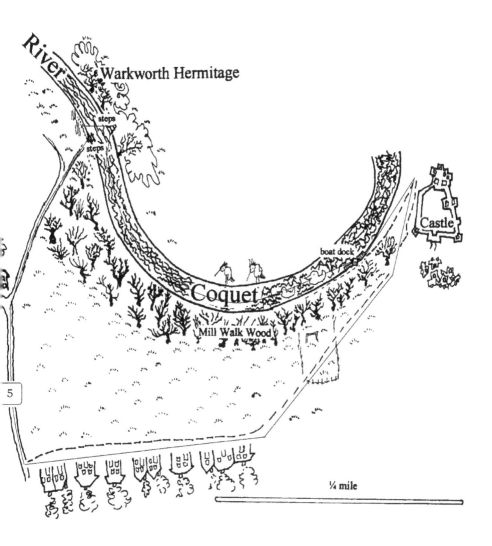

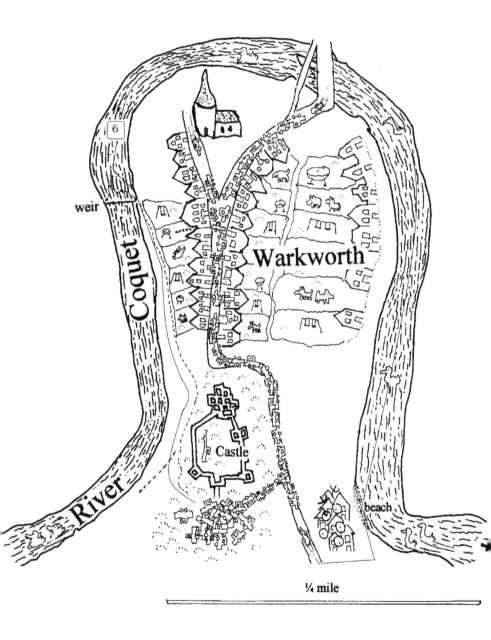

weir

Coquet

River

6

Warkworth

Castle

beach

¼ mile

5. Warkworth Hermitage

Back in the Middle Ages the Percy family decided to have a hermit in the same way that you might decide to have a cleaning lady or a gardener. They installed him near their castle in a cave on the far side of the Coquet Estuary and told him to pray for them. The cave is still there and by all accounts its interior is a marvellous sight to behold. But it is open only intermittently over the summer when English Heritage runs a ferry for visitors. For the rest of the year the cave is locked and barred. If you want to see the outside of the Hermitage, however, there is nothing to stop you from popping along at any time. (The sign that says 'No pleasure craft to land here', does not, of course, apply to swimhikers.)

From Warkworth Castle take the field path that runs southwest, then west by gardens. to a minor road-cum-path. Take this track north to a beautiful meadow on the edge of the river. On the far back is an enticing scene, with weathered sandstone cliffs moulded into curves and old yews lining the bank. Hidden behind one of these yews, lies the Hermitage.

Unless the tide is high, enter the water about ten yards higher up from the steps on the near bank. This will compensate for the current downstream and allow you to gain the steps on the far bank. Take the path west to the Hermitage and admire what can be seen from the outside (a torch might help for peering in). The cave has worked windows and natural sandstone holes. Abutting the cave is a ruined building with a great fireplace.

Return to the steps and swim down the river past Mill Walk Wood. There are cormorants and herons and eider ducks (the male ducks looking rather like penguins that have learned to fly). Exit at the boat dock with a little hut. From the dock, a path slopes up to beneath the western walls of the castle.

6. The Warkworth Loop

Below the Hermitage the picturesque village of Warkworth is contained in a loop of the River Coquet. The main street is remarkably pretty, although it has the misfortune to also be the A1018. At one end of the street is a fourteenth century bridge and the ancient Church of St. Lawrence, at the other end is the Percys' castle, with its stone lions carved into the walls and its maze-like keep.*

There is no better way to see Warkworth Village than to swim around it. From the entrance to the castle take the path north by back garden walls to the weir. As the river is an estuary, the weir may or may not be visible depending on the tide (to go with the flow the tide should be quite low). Slide down the bank, wade in and start swimming. For 50 yards the water is shallow and fast, then it is generally deep and slow, although you may bump your knee once or twice. The loop takes you past the church and the stone houses of Warkworth on the right hand bank while on the left there are woods and cliffs. Half way round there is a double bridge where the water runs quickly, keep to the left bank for the slower water.

The exit is on the right bank, a sand and mud beach by the new houses, just before the river bends away. You will have to counteract a moderate pull towards the left bank. From the beach take the path and road back up to the castle.

---

* From this castle brave Harry Hotspur left his ladylove to embark on his fatal rebellion against Henry IV. As he rode south, Hotspur's co-conspirators got cold feet, leaving him to die alone at the hands of the oafish and *lumpen* Prince Harry.

The river pulls you along at a gentle pace. There are ducks and swans for company.[*] What could be nicer? You will find yourself thinking: 'Why get out? I think I will drift all the way down to the sea'. Resist this temptation and do not miss your exit! If you do, you may, depending on the state of the tide, fall over a four-foot high weir.

---

[*] And apparently sometimes a seal.

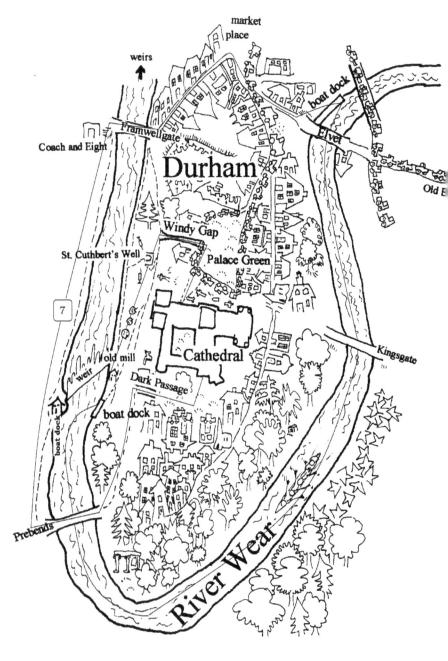

market place

weirs

boat dock

Coach and Eight

Framwellgate

Elvet

Durham

Old E

Windy Gap

St. Cuthbert's Well

Palace Green

7

Kingsgate

old mill

weir

Cathedral

Dark Passage

boat dock

boat dock

Prebends

River Wear

½ mile

7. The Durham Loop[*]

Like Warkworth, the city of Durham is contained in the loop of a river, in this case the River Wear, and the best way to see it is to take a swimhike.

Start at the Coach and Eight's[**] smelly steps that lead up from the riverbank to the southwest side of ancient Framwellgate Bridge. Cross the bridge, skirt above the market square and find Elvet Bridge, a fine old stone bridge. Do not cross this bridge. Instead, take the steps down to the hired boat dock and swim underneath it. As you continue downsteam you will swim under two more bridges. Kingsgate, a modern high-level pedestrian bridge, has won an award from the Concrete Association. Despite this dubious accolade the bridge is actually quite nice. You then enter a beautiful stretch with high banks of ivy clad trees. There are no hermit's caves here, but there are ice house hideaways and grunt holes.[***] Watch for kingfishers, swift lines of blue above the river. At the bend the current slows as water backs up from the weir and Prebends Bridge, the most picturesque bridge in Durham, comes into view. Swim beneath its arches and exit on the boat dock on the Cathedral side 200 yards below the bridge and just above the weir.

There is now a choice of three routes to the Cathedral.

(1) The most direct route heads diagonally up from the boat dock, past the old mill (now a museum), to emerge directly underneath the Cathedral. This path has been 'temporarily' closed, perhaps until it becomes so overgrown and dilapidated

---

[*] *Note to 2nd Edn* A shorter version of this route can be seen on Youtube: PTandN, 'durham swimhike june 2011'.
[**] *Note to 2nd Edn* This pub is now rebranded as some other name.
[***] A guide book to Britain's grunt holes is surely long overdue.

that it can be permanently closed.[*] Half way up the path, wild strawberries provide respite from the thorns and nettles.

(2) A little further down the river, a second path goes straight up to the Cathedral via St. Cuthbert's Well. This path to the ancient source of water for the inhabitants of Durham has been fenced off because it is steep. The public have meekly accepted this abrogation of their rights and no longer visit the massive stone font built into the side of the hill with its half legible Latin inscription:

FONS: CUTHBERT
1600

The drug addicts of Durham, however, are made of sterner stuff and have made St. Cuthbert's Well their own. Hypodermic needles and other detritus are scattered liberally around, and the walls have been assiduously graffitied. A large roll of silver foil is balanced carefully upright in the recess of the font to keep it safe and dry. The water streaming from the well is drinkable, and indeed quite tasty. Let us hope that it retains its curative properties.

The more intrepid swimhiker will make it up one or other of these paths somehow, but if you would prefer not to have to struggle there is a less direct third option.

(3) Follow the riverbank path downstream almost until Framwellgate Bridge before switching back up a broad, gradually sloping track.

---

[*] *Note to 2nd Edn* Somewhat to my surprise, the path is now open again.

Whichever route you chose, take Windy Gap to Palace Green and enter the Cathedral by its front entrance. The cathedral has an enormous pair of knockers; one of them, a replica is affixed to this door, while the original is on display inside.

With a touching faith in human nature the ecclesiastics of Durham Cathedral rely upon the generosity of their visitors rather than imposing a fee upon them. Please swimhikers, help to justify their faith! Let the sight of someone dripping with riverwater, a swimsac slung carelessly over their shoulder, have the beadles and vergers at the door beaming with delighted anticipation.

Wander amongst the massive pillars; the Cathedral is an early experiment and the architects do not yet realise how thin they can make them. The overall feel of the place is not so much soaring, delicate and beautiful as big, thick and lumpy. Beneath the lectern the pelican bites its breast to feed its young. Beneath the choir stalls are misericords of peacocks; mermaids; a pig playing the harp, but they are roped off. Behind the choir are the remains of St. Cuthbert, which at some point got mixed up with the head of King Oswald. In the middle ages women who ventured into the Cathedral were set upon by sadistic Benedictines, ostensibly to protect Cuthbert's pure flesh—miraculously whole—from being corrupted. In the end a separate woman's chamber, the Galilee Chapel, had to be tacked on at the back.[*]

---

[*] A woman must have got to Cuthbert eventually because when his coffin was opened, in 1827, all that was left was his skeleton. *Note to 2nd Edn* If, indeed, this *was* Cuthbert. Local legend has it that Cuthbert's body was swapped for another at the time of Henry VIII, and removed to a secret place that was—and is—known only to The Three.

If the tower is open it is well worth the modest entry price. The steps start broad straight and easy but they become progressively smaller steeper and more uneven and wind ever more tightly until they almost disappear into the core of the spiral. The stairs also twist first one way, and then the other, so that at the very heart of this most ancient cathedral there lies a representation of the building block of life: the double helix.

Eventually you reach the top and have a marvellous view, but how will you get down again, or rather, what will you do when you meet someone coming up the other way?

Leave the Cathedral by the back entrance. Go down Dark Passage and over Prebends Bridge. Take the path along the riverbank enjoying the famous view across the weir. It returns you to the smelly steps at Framwellgate Bridge.

8. Durham Assize Court

A second Durham City route of about the same distance follows the higher section of the river. From the Assize Court go out of town to the junction of Old Elvet and Green Lane. Take the path round the cricket field and beneath Maiden Castle Wood. There is a steep entry to the River Wear about 50 yards below the footbridge.* At first the water is shallow and you may need to wade before swimming round the broad curve of the river. Exit at the boat step on the left bank 100 yards above the footbridge. Here you can either explore the river banks and Cathedral, before returning to the Assize Court over Kingsgate Bridge, or simply return directly up a vennel to the Court.

Vennels are a feature of Durham. Behind the cobbled streets crowded with shoppers are a maze of empty narrow passageways, some descending steeply through low doorways to the river, others hemmed in by high walls overhung with razor wire, lead you from cosy historical drama to film noir in a few steps. This particular vennel skirts the wonderful old brick public swimming pool, with its high church-like windows. Like so many wonderful old swimming pools, this one is about to be discarded for a new one being built lower down the river. What will happen to the old pool?** Occasionally they become private pools, but at least then the pool is still used. More often, the façade is retained, the pool is filled in and the building is turned onto a block of flats. In one small town near Durham the old public pool was turned into a brothel.

---

* *Note to 2ⁿᵈ Edn* There is now a boat dock at the footbridge.
** *Note to 2ⁿᵈ Edn* It is now derelict.

Durham Assize Court is an imposing building, with its own special place in the history of swimhiking. In 2002 I was summoned to court as a juror. I was quietly excited, keen to do my civic duty. I think all of us new jurors were. We were welcomed; we were shown a video; we were shown inside an empty court room. Then we were escorted to the holding pen, where we perched expectantly on plastic seats waiting in eager anticipation to be called in to free the innocent and to hang the guilty.

To preserve the illusion that justice is reasonable, there is a rule that you are not allowed to say what happened in a jury room. But this rule, does not, I believe, apply if nothing happens at all. We sat in that stuffy little room for two weeks, and not once were we ever called into court. It was like waiting for a train that never came. Some people played cards, some people read, some people watched TV, some people stared vacantly into space.

The windows to the jury room were barred and frosted, but outside spring was bursting into life with swallows swooping above the slow brown river. I felt a deep yearning to be free. If only I could be running and swimming outside! With this feeling in my heart, I used the time to turn the vague concept of the swimsac into a set of detailed plans, and prepared the first draft of a patent application. The swimsac is very simple, but I had plenty of time to think, and after due consideration made a list of seventy eight claims for my invention. I sent it off to the patent office and, after some correspondence, they accepted forty seven of them. The patent is registered as GB 2 392 375 B.

An Otter

I knew there were otters about in Durham. One night they had been caught on CCTV exploring the Market Square right in the centre of the town, and another night they had climbed the hill and eaten all the fish in my neighbour's pond. But despite getting up almost every morning to go swimming or swimhiking in the Wear in the quiet of first light, I had never seen one. Sometimes I heard a suggestive splash. But that was it.

When I finally get to see an otter, it is in the middle of the day, the first warm day of spring, a day when everyone is out and about. My wife and I are walking along the riverbank and a dog is sniffing along behind us. It is not our dog, it just seems to prefer us to its owner, who is some way back. My wife is not especially keen on dogs, so I take my chance. 'Turn off here'! I say. 'We'll let it pass'.

We have stepped onto a little track down to Matt's Beach—a tiny beach with deep water that is hidden from the path. I know it well having swam there hundreds of times. 'Hmm'! I exclaim, as if in surprise at what we have found. 'Well, I suppose, as we're here, perhaps I'll just have a quick dip...' My wife sighs and waits patiently while I strip and wade into the water.

As I am dressing again, I become aware of something almost immediately below me in the water, beneath the willow bush that grows out over the river. From what I can see it looks like a large fish. But would a large fish nibble at the branches like that? I fumble to put my glasses on. It's an otter! My first sight of an otter in England! And at my favourite little swimming beach too. What a momentous occasion! For a few seconds we have a marvellous view, then the otter tucks itself away against the bank so that it is hidden by the overhanging branches. I can still hear it though, and perhaps if we stay very quiet and still it will…

At this point the owner of the dog turns up. 'Hello mate'! he calls down to me. 'I'm looking for a red dog toy. Have you seen it floating by'?

'No'.

This reply does not satisfy the man. He scans the bushes; conveys a sense of the urgency and importance of reclaiming his dog toy; seems reluctant to believe that we have not seen it; suspects, perhaps, that we are hiding it from him. He comes down and peers around everywhere, all the while talking loudly about the dog toy.

'But we've seen an otter'! my wife says.

The man is not interested. Only his dog toy interests him. It is shaped like a bone. It must be around somewhere.

Eventually and reluctantly the man departs to scour the banks downriver. Now I can now no longer hear the otter. Could it still be there, lying low? There *is* something there. I look carefully between the branches. What is that? I can see *something*, something red. It is shaped like a bone. It is the dog toy.

I do not call the man back. I thought the otter might like to play with it.

Bubbles

It is an early Sunday morning in June, and I am swimhiking down the Wear from Kingsgate Bridge in Durham. The banks are quiet, with just the occasional jogger and one sleeping fisherman. Swimming beneath Prebends Bridge, I am slightly annoyed that someone has parked their car right on the footpath by the left bank boat dock, but mainly I am intrigued by the bubbles. They are breaking the surface in a series of powerful surges, rising three or four inches high. They are not continuous, but are frequent, erupting every few seconds. Could it be bubbles from a big fish? No, there is something unnatural about them. So what is it? Vaguely I remember the letter from United Utilities about their 'bubble mixers' in Thirlmere. Probably they are something like that. I am not quite sure why anyone should put such things in the River Wear, but still, there they are and now is my chance to enjoy playing with them! I double back, swim straight for the bubbles and plant myself on top of them. Bubble Bubble Bubble! Ha Ha Ha! How odd, and how amusing, a bit like a jacuzzi. What fun!

I look down; I can see something lighter coloured and squarish in the water below. Then I feel a sharp pinch on my leg.

Startled I swim away. 'What the hell is that'? I ask the empty river.

I get out at the boat dock on the right bank and get changed. On the left bank a man in a wetsuit heaves himself out of the water. He has a pack on his back and, for an amazed second, I think he could be another swimhiker. But no. It is an oxygen pack. He must be a diver, and the bubbles....Hmm.

We look at each other curiously. At least, I am curious. I finish getting changed and run over the bridge to say hello, apologise, and perhaps make a new friend. He is still there, now in a tracksuit, going to and fro. But when I get close, he gets in his car and shuts the door.

I am left with unanswered questions. But they are answered soon enough. According to local legend, Archbishop Michael Ramsey, after he retired, went to Prebends Bridge and threw all his worldly baubles in the river. I knew of the Archbishop's decision and respected it; a gold cross that I saw glistering in the Wear I left in place. (My nobility in this matter is tarnished only slightly by my first deciding that it only *looked* gold.) The diver knew the story too, and was busy fishing all the stuff out again (not for personal gain, I hasten to add, but to restore it to the Church). And not just Archbishop Ramsey's paraphernalia was being recovered. Prebends Bridge is in a breathtakingly beautiful location and for hundreds of years people, when they are heartbroken, have come there with their rings and other precious keepsakes and consigned them to the waters. He fished these out as well, and they were all proudly put on display in an exhibition at Palace Green, where it was explained that people had dropped them in accidentally.

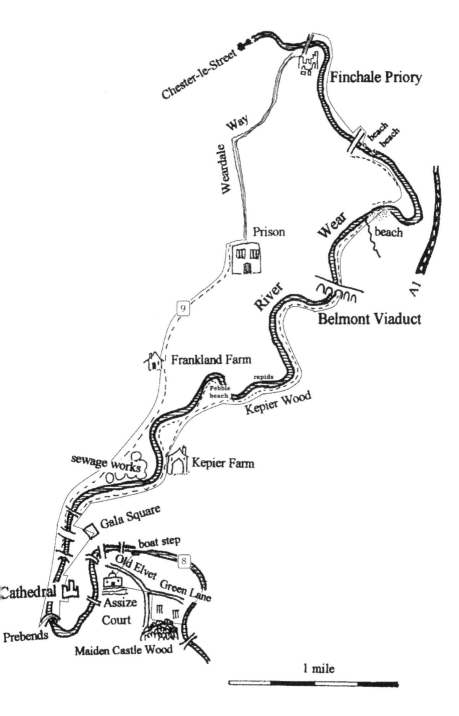

9. Durham Cathedral to Finchale Priory

This swimhike follows the course of the River Wear downstream and returns across country. Aside from two river crossings the hike is wholly on foot unless you choose to do some extra swimming in the deeper slower stretches. (The best of these is a 300 yard stretch from the pebble beach at the field just above Kepier Wood to the rapids.)

From the front entrance of Durham Cathedral descend through Windy Gap to the Marketplace, Gala Square and to the right bank of the river. Past the vaulted entrance to Kepier Farm you have a choice of following the bending river or shortcutting on a straight field path. The paths rejoin in the well spaced oaks of Kepier Wood. Towering ahead is Belmont Viaduct, almost as high as Durham Cathedral and considerably more graceful. Go *beneath* Belmont Viaduct.

For many years, walkers exploring the river, have all had exactly the same thought:

'My! What a fine bridge, I'd rather like to walk across that'.

Easier said than done! It is not easy to get from the banks of the Wear to the start of the bridge, but by backtracking through the woods, or scrambling up the bare earth clinging to tree roots, the more agile have somehow made it up and, exhausted and dirty but full of excitement, set out to cross the viaduct. There an awful disappointment awaits. The County Council has anticipated their thoughts and, with brutal efficiency, set out to thwart them.* It has shut off the entrance

---

* The County Council squats on a hill above the city, but its tentacles of power grope ever outwards. In 2008 it swallowed up the district councils. Not surprisingly, in a referendum on the issue 76% of voters

to the viaduct with a high metal three-spiked-fence. The fence
is coated in a viscous anti-climb paint and sticks out for
several feet at each side, with a fatal fall beneath. There is
also a warning notice, rather redundant in the circumstances,
to keep off.* But all this ought to change, for in December
2007 Sustrans won a popular TV vote to get 50 million pounds
of heritage lottery money. One of the things the cycling
charity says it will do with the cash is to renovate and reopen
Belmont Viaduct.

Sustrans is creating a fantastic off-road cycling network, but
no organisation is without its foibles and Sustrans has an
unfortunate penchant for knocking down nice old bridges,
leaving a gap for a year or two, and then filling it with an over-
engineered and sometimes quite ugly new bridge. Of course,
this is unthinkable for Belmont Bridge, but I am still suffering
from a recurring nightmare.

*A dour surveyor looks at the trees sprouting on the viaduct.
'This will have to come down'. Cranes and fluorescent
jackets. Bang, crash, bump. Now the struts are like left like
tree stumps. I cannot bear to look. There is a long wait. We
are in the future and a sinewey mess of metal cables, girders
and concrete has been slung across the river. This constitutes
the new 'bridge'. A politician cuts a ribbon, a crowd of*

were rather apprehensive about this, and voted to keep the districts.
But all to no avail. The referendum was dismissed as the 'so-called
referendum', while placemen trumpeted the diktat as 'great news for
the people of Durham'.
* *Note to 2nd Edn* Some public spirited citizen subsequently made a
small gap at the base of this fence and thereby re-opened the bridge, at
least to anyone who was willing to crawl on their back like a caterpillar
to get in. Unfortunately, the Council noticed and it is now sealed off
again.

*school children—all wearing cycling helmets—are being told
to cheer. I am at the back of the crowd, shouting 'No!'. But
I cannot get through. 'No! No! No'!*

I jerk awake, my brow covered with beads of sweat 'like
bubbles in a late-disturbed stream'.

I am sure this will not happen. In fact, I doubt that anything
very much will happen anytime soon. I merely entertain the
modest hope that Sustrans will manage to get the job done
before I am dead.* It is indubitably a much better use of lottery
money than destroying Lake District paths under footways,
although quite why it should cost countless millions to reopen the bridge I find unclear. Why not simply take the fence
down?

Once beneath the viaduct continue along the path down the
right bank of the river until you come to a dead end at a stream
and a fence. Perversely, the path terminates at the start of the
most beautiful part of the river, where a meadow borders its
banks with a substantial sandy beach. The only fly in the
ointment is the proximity of the A1 motorway.

Make your way to the beach (you may have to share it with
cows), and swim straight across to the quarried crags on the
left shore (now part of a children's adventure farm). Take the
bulldozed track to the field, cross to the gate and follow the
track down the left bank. Look out for a pedestrian bridge; it
is difficult to spot through the foliage, but you will realise that
you are close when the track bends away from the river. This
bridge has also been enthusiastically sealed off, albeit without

---

* *Note to 2nd Edn* Now I just hope that the bridge will not fall down
before I am dead.

quite the same degree of deadly thoroughness as at the viaduct. However, 100 yards *above* the bridge is a rock platform where you can enter the river and swim to the right bank. There is a choice of two sandy beaches to land on. One is directly opposite, but there is no need to pull across the current; if you allow yourself to drift downstream, a second beach, concealed by trees, lies just 20 yards above the bridge.

Make your way down the right bank to Finchale and cross the footbridge. The bridge takes you to the remains of Finchale Priory, home to the old pirate Saint Godric who arrived there after dreaming that Saint Cuthbert had told him to. Saint Godric prayed up to his neck in the river, which means that he must also have been swimming because, in moving water at that depth, you have to. Outside opening hours the ruins can be seen though the fence.

Return to Durham along the 'Weardale Way', past the Prison, Frankland Farm and the sewage works to Prebends Bridge. The Dark Passage takes you back to the Cathedral.

The Legend of the Worm
As the River Wear continues towards the sea from Finchale Priory there are further opportunities for swimhiking at the southern side of Chester-le-Street Park. Check your exit points. The river can flow fast here and towards the middle of the park, notices warn of drownings. Once below Chester-le-Street, the Wear disappears into Lambton Park. The Estate lies at the very heart of the North East and could have been its jewel in the crown. But the Estate is closed.

Lambton Park is, of course, the lair of the Lambton Worm. According to the ancient song, it was here that Young

Lambton fought and vanquished the worm-beast that rose up from the well. It must be added, however, that when tongues are loosened amongst the tight lipped folk that live in the grim shadow of the estate's perimeter wall, you may also hear a second, darker legend, foul and bestial, wherein victory was gained by the Worm and his descendants.

Some owners of the great estates that lie amidst England's cities have opened their grounds, or large parts of them, to visitors. Motorists pay a reasonable fee while those on foot can usually enter free. This is a tremendous boon to an area; the inhabitants of the surrounding towns becoming noticeably happier and more expansive. It is not that they visit the grounds all the time, but they know that if they want to, they

can. The shining example is Chatsworth, opened by the Duke and Duchess of Devonshire.

If only Lord Worm would follow their lead.*

---

* *Note to 2ⁿᵈ Edn* After his unseemly private life was revealed to a shocked public (with the help of a tiny camera and tape recorder hidden in a teddy bear), Lord Worm left Lambton and holed up a new lair in Italy. Here he grew to a ripe and unrepentant old age and died. Numerous offspring then went writhing through the courts in a protracted dispute over who would get what. Now there is talk of building houses on the estate and even opening the place up, a bit. But it remains shut.

Bamburgh

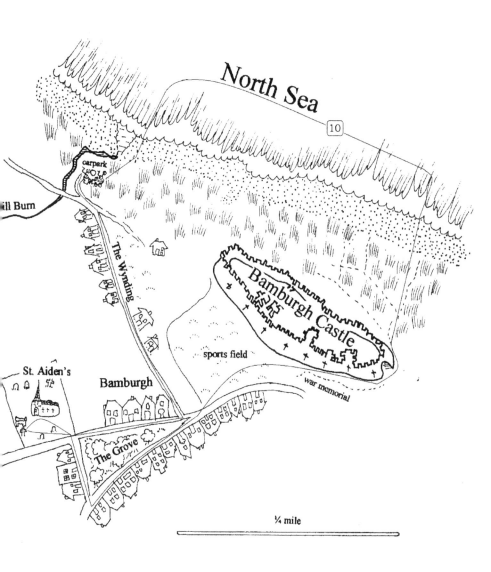

North Sea

10

carpark

ill Burn

The Wynding

St. Aiden's

Bamburgh

Bamburgh Castle

sports field

war memorial

The Grove

¼ mile

10. Bamburgh Castle

Mill Burn just north of Bamburgh has a small carpark for the surfers, photographers and dogwalkers that flock there. Head straight for the water and swim out beyond the breakers and then south parallel to the beach. There is an amazing view. On one side is the fine white sand, the dunes and the massive Castle on the rock. On the other side, lying low in the water and looking vaguely like oil tankers, are the Farne Islands. The islands provided a home, for a time, for Saint Cuthbert and for Grace Darling. Exit on the beach at the southern end of Bamburgh Castle. Someone's dogs will probably come and bark at you.

There are several paths through the dunes that emerge beneath the castle entrance (open 10-5). From the entrance a path takes you to the war memorial and sports field. Cross the field and explore the village before returning down the Wynding to Mill Burn. However, if like me you have an obsessive desire to avoid doglegs, you will not be satisfied with the vague suggestion to wander round and enjoy yourself. You will be asking anxiously:

'How can I visit the village highpoints *without once crossing my tracks*'?

This is how: first follow the southern side of Bamburgh's main street. Cross the Grove to enter St. Aiden's Churchyard. Here Grace Darling lies in stone beneath a canopy, nearby is the Darling family plot where she is buried. Return down the northern side of the street to join the Wynding.

The Channel

Why not swim from Bamburgh to the Farne Islands? Inner Farne is, after all, barely a mile off shore. In my case the answer is simple:

'I could do, but I am too frightened to'.

Mainly I am afraid of the seagulls that no doubt lurk on the islands waiting to attack, but I am also a little bit scared of drowning. It would be completely different if I had a boat to accompany me of course. Then it would be easy, I could laugh at the seagulls and if a current pulled me out to sea, I could just clamber into the boat. But this would also be dissatisfying as with a boat alongside you the swimsac—and indeed swimming—loses its purpose.

Why not swim the English Channel with a swimsac? In my case the answer is simple.

'I can't. I am not good enough to'.

But what if I *was* good enough to swim it? Again, I would be stuck: I would be too frightened—with good reason—to attempt it unsupported, but would not actually want to be followed by a boat.

What if someone else, a better swimmer and brave, if not foolhardy, attempts swim the Channel with just a swimsac, or even just a swimsuit with a passport and some euros tucked inside, what then? It would be a perilous undertaking, and is *emphatically not recommended*. In 1954 Ted May set out alone across the Channel towing an inner tube containing food and drink, and that was the last anyone ever heard of him. But if someone survived the attempt to swim across without a boat, and indeed succeeded, then I fear that a great injustice would await them.

Every hero needs a certificate to prove it, but the Channel Swimmer's Association would, I am fairly sure, refuse to supply one. The unaccompanied swimmer would have violated the rules in one way or another. A wetsuit would certainly disqualify them and a swimsac, even if not explicitly mentioned in the rules, would probably disqualify them too. And not having an official boat and an official from the Channel Swimmer's Association, would disqualify them, and not having been authorised in advance by the Channel Swimmer's Association would also disqualify them. The Channel Swimming and Piloting Federation, seems marginally less up tight and might possibly sell them some kind of certificate, but I am doubtful.

My solution to this problem is to offer anyone who swims the Channel without a boat a homemade certificate from me. Furthermore, they will not need to pay the rather steep fees charged by the above two associations as I will provide it *for nothing*. I will also put them on an official list. They may not be on the other official lists, but there again, all previous Channel swimmers (so far as I am aware) are excluded from *my* list on the grounds that they have cheated by having a boat with them.

Embleton Bay

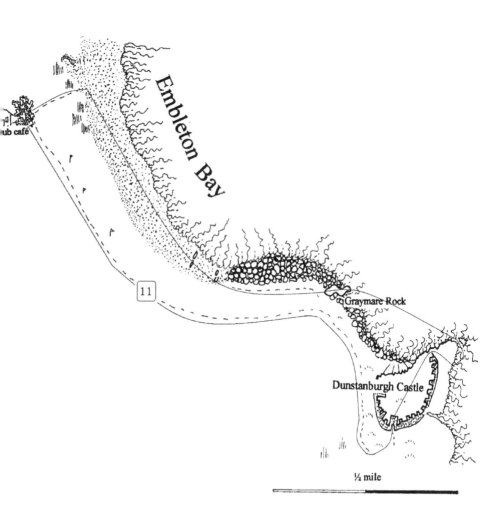

ub café

Embleton Bay

11

Graymare Rock

Dunstanburgh Castle

¼ mile

11. Dunstanburgh Castle

> The whitening breakers sound so near,
> Where, boiling through the rocks, they roar,
> On Dunstanborough's cavern'd shore[*]

It is not always like that of course, but this route is only to be undertaken in calm weather.

From the Golf Club and public café at the end of Embleton village go east through the sand dunes to Embleton Bay. To the south the ruins of the castle stand above the Bay. Take the beach and dune path south to mount Graymare Rock, which curves like a gentle wave into the water. Swim east for the point below the castle. Beneath the water, at first, are large round stones and seaweed, above the sheer cliff gradually descends to the point. Curious cormorants circle and swoop low overhead, before plopping heavily into the water.

As you approach the point the pull of the tide which, if taken on the ebb, will have been helping you out of the bay, clashes with the main northerly current making the water more choppy. With the tide low you see that there is a rocky island at the end of the point, swim through the channel and climb out. The far side of the peninsula is one long rock platform bounded to the south by a small bay, with many easy points to exit.

Enter the castle grounds through the gap in the wall near the point. There is a wide expanse of grass; remains of walls; the

---

[*] Walter Scott, *Marmion*, Canto II, The Convent

Keep perched on fingers of rock; the Gatehouse with its arched doorway. This entrance—or in our case exit—is guarded by a ticket booth so remember to bring some change. (Leaving the castle by land outside regular visiting hours presents little difficulty.)

Take the path back beneath the Keep and almost to Greymare Rock before cutting inland and returning over the golf course to the clubhouse.

Poets and Saints

Samuel Taylor Coleridge kept an eye open for a good bathing pool on his hikes around Keswick, and described his ecstatic pleasure at swimming in the sea:

> Dreams (the soul herself forsaking)
> Tearful raptures, boyish mirth;
> Silent adorations making
> A blessed shadow of this Earth![*]

Apart from the bit about tearful raptures and boyish mirth, I am not sure what all this means, but obviously Coleridge was enjoying the water, and he was not the only romantic poet to do so. Byron swam across the Hellespont (which sounds ideal for a swimsac), and Shelley drowned.

The intensity of the experience of nature and of God that entranced Coleridge, surely also inspired the British saints. Their practice of praying up to their neck in water is taken as a mortification, but I think it more likely that they took a pleasure in swimming and that the act of swimming was an

---

[*] *On Revisiting the Sea-Shore*

act of prayer. The mortification idea was probably put about
by the ancestors of people who, today, say 'you must be mad'
every time they see a swimmer enter the water.

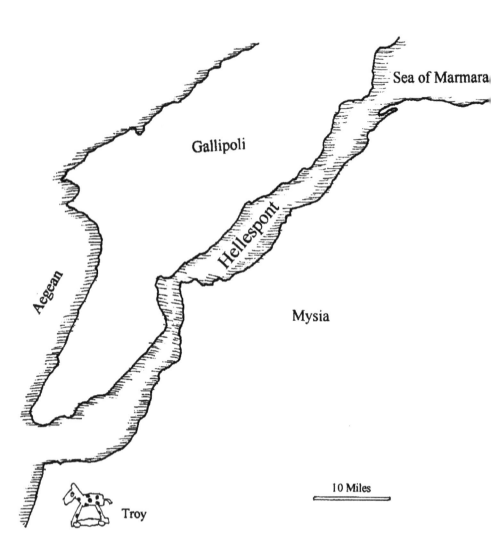

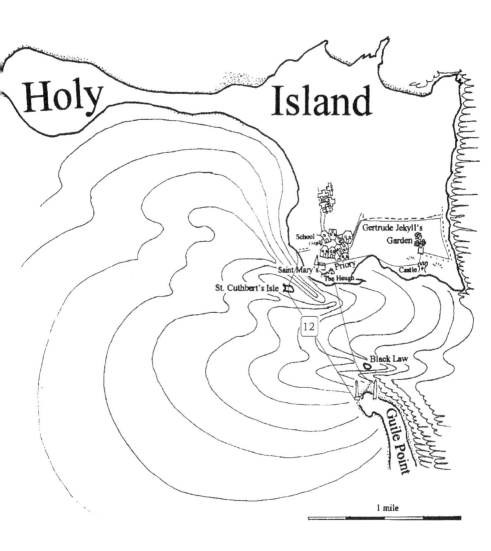

Holy Island

School

Gertrude Jekyll's Garden

Saint Mary's

Priory

St. Cuthbert's Isle

The Heugh

Castle

12

Black Law

Guile Point

1 mile

12. Holy Island

And so at last to Holy Island or Lindisfarne, the one-time home of Saint Cuthbert. The Saint appears everywhere in the North East: his bones lie in Durham Cathedral his Farne Island home lies across the sea from Bamburgh. Even in the Lake District we have been paddling in his wake. In our very first swimhike across Derwentwater we visited the island hermitage of Cuthbert's friend Saint Herbert, and it was Cuthbert, if you remember, who arranged for them both to die on the same day.

> The monks of Lindisfarne meanwhile
> Were gazing on their dead:
> At that same hour, in Derwent Isle,
> A kindred soul had fled.[*]

St. Cuthbert was drawn to water. He would go in up to the neck to pray and hence, doubtless, to swim. On one occasion Cuthbert came out of the sea accompanied by a couple of otters who frolicked around him on the shore. He was rather embarrassed about the fact, and ordered the monk who saw the whole thing not to tell anyone until after was dead.[**] The conclusion is obvious. Saint Cuthbert had not just been praying in the water, he had also been playing with the otters.

The Monastery at Holy Island was not quite isolated enough for St. Cuthbert; he lived in a little chapel on another island, now called St. Cuthbert's Isle, which is connected to the main island only at low tide. This island is our first destination.

---

[*] Wordsworth
[**] Bede, *The Life of St. Cuthbert*, Ch. 10.

From the village centre on Holy Island, go east down the road to the school and then take the path east to the edge of the stony beach. There is a fixed rope to help you down the final muddy, grassy slope to the rocks. Depending on the state of the tide you can walk, wade or swim to St. Cuthbert's Isle.

I arrived, with a full wetsuit, early on a summer's morning. The beach was not quiet, the whole bay noisy with moaning birds, the sound was loud and ghostly. The tide was half way in so I swam the narrow channel to the small grassy island. A little overgrown square of foundation stones are all that are left of the chapel.

Where now? The incoming seawater flows south through the channel and east along the shore of Holy Island. If you are without a wetsuit, or do not want lots of wildlife in your face, you might swim east with the flow for about 200 yards and then rejoin the beach at Holy Island beneath the priory.

I swim south for the more westerly of the two obelisks at Guile Point. It feels a long way. Plovers with sharp scissor tails plunge into the water all around as they fish. There are bubbles in the water and then a head pops up. It is a seal. How charming. One or two more appear. Now there is a whole family of seals swimming in Loch Ness Monster formation, one at the front with its head up, the others undulating through the water in a line behind. They break ranks to raise their heads and look at me, destroying the illusion.

Suddenly seal heads are popping up and down everywhere like a fairground game. There must be twenty of them.

Splash! One jumps out of the water close behind. Splash! now to the side.

The obelisk, deceptively close because it is so tall, takes a long time to reach. No mention of its maker (John Dobson, early nineteenth century), but someone who restored it in the 1950s has put a stone plaque on the side announcing his name and that of his assistant. Behind, the platform of the obelisk, the seagrass that edges the shore is surrounded by a low electric fence encircling nesting boxes for puffins.

On the map it appears that you could almost walk back to Holy Island at low tide, but with the tide rising the rocky reefs are rapidly vanishing and Black Law, the small island north of Guile Point, is already cut off. I swim through the shallow channel towards it. A forceful current pushes me west around the edge. I go with the flow. In any event the island is not very inviting, it is full of terns and has another electric fence. I swim for the Priory, the top of its ruins visible behind the Heugh. More seals pop up.

Splash!

Splash! Splash! Splash!

One large seal is jumping repeatedly within a couple of yards of me, landing with great belly flops. Am I being played with, threatened, courted? What would Saint Cuthbert have done? Then a puffin! Soon they are everywhere paddling on the water and flying past.

I crawl up the rocky beach a little before seven in the morning, back on Holy Island after almost an hour and a half in the water. It has been an intense experience. Four people and a dog are at the top of the path staring down at me as I get changed. Oh good! I can have a chat. I turn towards them. They all hurry away.

If you have time, it would be delightful to spend the rest of the day lazily exploring this wonderful island. But if you must rush to drive back across the causeway before the island is cut off, where can you go? From the beach take the path to the entrance of the Priory and to Saint Mary's Church--very still and silent after the noise of the birds. Then follow the path toward Lindisfarne Castle and turn off to Gertrude Jekyll's Garden, a small walled oasis. Continue east to the open sea, then turn north to enjoy six hundred yards of wild coast before returning to the village down a farm track. You had better run. The island is festooned with warning photographs of what will happen to your car if you are caught by the tide.[*]

---

[*] I cannot help but add that the unfortunate car depicted is an off road vehicle.

Goodbye and an Invitation

We have reached the end of our adventures in the Lake District and North East England. But as for swimhiking, it is only the beginning. Where next?

On long winter evenings I like nothing better than to spread out maps of Scotland. What fantastic routes lie in store for the intrepid swimhiker! The long lochs, the deep rivers, the islands—hundreds of possibilities leap to the eye like jumping salmon. And what adventures might there be? Frolicsome otters, rutting stags, friendly ghillies?

'Darling'?

'What'?

'Would you like to go to Scotland for our next holiday? We could visit a kilt factory'.

'No thank you. I would rather go on a package holiday to the Mediterranean'.

The Mediterranean! Why not? The water is warm, there are inlets, islands, cliffs, arches and lots of colourful fish. There are adventures too, with 'private' beaches to invade and large schools of small brown jellyfish to get stuck in the middle of.

But then I realise that the whole world is teaming with uncharted territory waiting to be explored by the swimhiker. I need to go *everywhere*!

So already in my head I have planned the three next books:

Swimhiking in Scotland
Swimhiking at the Mediterranean
Swimhiking around the World

On sober reflection, these plans hit a snag. Scotland is much bigger than the Lake District and North East England, and is also further away from where I live. It will take me at least twenty years to write the Scotland book. The Mediterranean is bigger still. I had better allow myself about forty years for that. The world is also very big, so let us say sixty years. Now even if I manage to achieve all these tasks concurrently, by the time I have finished I will be 104.

For the solution to this problem I turn to you the reader. You will, I hope, have been inspired to go swimhiking yourself. So why not write about it too? If you think that you have discovered a good route describe it, identify its checkpoints, say something about what it is like, draw a map, and send it to me. (Remember that a good route is not the same as an arduous or dangerous route, a simple and easy swimhike can be very satisfying.) I will place the routes I receive in one of the three categories: Scotland, the Mediterranean, the World, and when I get enough routes I will publish them.

At this point you might be asking:

'Oh Yeah. And how much money are you going to pay me for writing *your* next book'?

I will tell you: *I will pay you nothing.* Indeed the economics are such that you will probably not even get a free copy, although you might get a discount. But let us not squabble. Let me just say that I will be delighted to hear from anyone about their adventures with a swimsac. Have fun and please be careful.

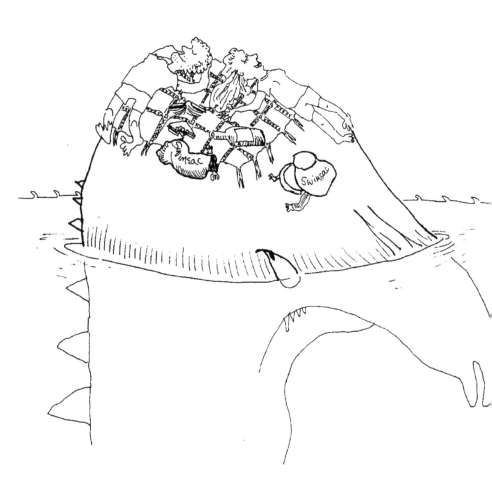

APPENDIX

Swimsacs and the Laws of Physics

There is no substitute for trial and error in understanding the load carrying potential of a swimsac. However, when dealing with heavy loads, too much in the way of error means that the bag will sink and, unless you unstrap it, so will you. With this in mind, some rules based on elementary physics help in providing a framework for deciding whether or not you are safe to step into the water. These rules are not precise (for example they assume that water density is a constant where in fact it varies), but they do give rough and ready answers to three basic questions about what happens when a heavy load is placed in a swimsac.

Q. 1. Will the swimsac float?

Rule 1

A swimsac will float if the volume of the sac in litres is greater than the mass of the sac in kilos.

Explanation

Density = $\frac{\text{Mass}}{\text{Volume}}$

Fresh water has a density of 1. ie, it has a mass of 1 kilo per litre. If the swimsac has an average density of less than 1 it will float, if its density is greater than 1 it will sink.

Example

When fully loaded, the main compartment of a swimsac has a volume of 35 litres and a mass of 38 kilos. This gives it a density of 1.09. Therefore, the swimsac will sink unless its volume can be increased.

Inflatable pockets add to the overall volume of a swimsac without adding to its overall mass. (The mass of air is negligible and can be assumed to be zero.) A single 3 litre inflatable pocket would prevent the swimsac from sinking, by increasing its volume to 38 litres. This 3 litre pocket will give the swimsac a density of 1 and bring it into a state of equilibrium in the water.

Q. 2 What is the minimum safety margin for inflatable air pockets?

Rule 2
For safety, a swimsac must (a) have at least two equally sized air pockets. (b) Each air pocket must be at least the volume needed to bring the bag with a maximum load into a state of equilibrium in the water.

Explanation and Example
If one air pocket deflates in the water, the bag will be supported by the other. Thus a 35 litre sac with a maximum load of 38 kilos will need two 3 litre air pockets. This will give it an overall volume of 41 litres.

Q. 3 What proportion of the swimsac will be above the water?

Rule 3
The proportion of the swimsac above water is the ratio of its mass to its volume.

Explanation
The mass of the bag will displace the equivalent mass of water. The greater the volume, the more of the bag will remain out of the water.

Examples
(a) If a swimsac has a mass of 38 kilos and a total volume of 41 litres, then 38 divided by 41 = 0.93. The bag will be 93% submerged and 7 % above water.
(b) To increase the proportion of the 38 kilo bag out of the water to, say one quarter, the two air pockets could be increased in size from 3 litres to 7.83 litres each. This would increase the total volume of the sac from 41 litre to 50.66 litres. 38 kilos divided by 50.66 litres = 0.75. The bag will now be only 75% submerged.

The following graph illustrates these rules.

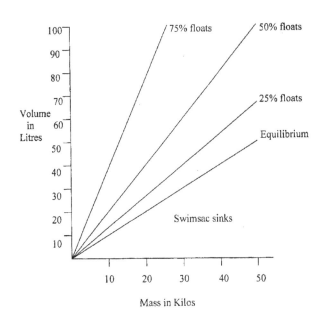

Density of a Swimsac